Focused Positivity

Focused Positivity

The Path to Success and Peace of Mind

John F. Tholen, PhD

ROWMAN & LITTLEFIELD
Lanham • Boulder • New York • London

Published by Rowman & Littlefield
An imprint of The Rowman & Littlefield Publishing Group, Inc.
4501 Forbes Boulevard, Suite 200, Lanham, Maryland 20706
www.rowman.com

86-90 Paul Street, London EC2A 4NE, United Kingdom

British Library Cataloguing in Publication Information Available

Library of Congress Cataloging-in-Publication Data

Names: Tholen, John F., author.
Title: Focused positivity : the path to success and peace of mind / John F. Tholen,
    PhD.
Description: Lanham : Rowman & Littlefield, [2021] | Includes bibliographical
    references. | Summary: "Focused Positivity is designed for anyone who suffers more
    anxiety or sadness than is justified by healthy concern or normal grieving. In other
    words, most of us. By helping readers identify and change self-talk, John F. Tholen
    creates the opportunity for a more productive and satisfying life by redirecting our
    attention to healthier thoughts"—Provided by publisher.
Identifiers: LCCN 2021014372 (print) | LCCN 2021014373 (ebook) | ISBN
    9781538153284 (cloth ; alk. paper) | ISBN 9781538153291 (epub)
Subjects: LCSH: Positive psychology. | Attitude (Psychology) | Optimism. | Self-talk.
    | Peace of mind. | Success.
Classification: LCC BF204.6 .T46 2021 (print) | LCC BF204.6 (ebook) | DDC
    150.19/88—dc23
LC record available at https://lccn.loc.gov/2021014372
LC ebook record available at https://lccn.loc.gov/2021014373

For Sandy, the love of my life
and everything I could have wanted
during our forty-one years of marriage.
And for our sons, Ben and Daniel,
and our grandchildren, Sloane and Grant,
all of whom have brought us such joy.

Disclaimer

No book can replace the services of a licensed physician or mental health professional. Although likely to serve as a useful adjunct to medical or mental health treatment, this book is not intended to be a cure or treatment for any injury, illness, or any other medical problem.

Contents

Author's Note

This book is based on thousands of notes I wrote for my psychology "patients" over the course of my more than forty years in clinical practice. Compiling them into this book has been complicated by the fact that I wrote each idea many times in different words. As a result, I have spent a great deal of time deleting or integrating repetitive paragraphs. As repetition can reinforce understanding and memory of a concept, however, I will own the duplication that remains.

Few, if any, of the ideas presented herein are original. *Focused Positivity* is primarily a "mash up" of psychological philosophy and what social science research has discovered about the relationship of our thoughts to our feelings and actions. At the end of each chapter I address the practical issue of "how" by stepping out of the first-person plural to present specific instructions, "steps" likely to enhance peace of mind and motivate constructive action.

I have provided a bibliography of the sources that have most contributed to the ideas I express but have not provided specific citations. This book is not intended to be a scholarly work. The information presented mainly reflects my accumulated knowledge and opinion, and the book is intended to persuade and guide the reader to healthier behavior patterns, not prove the accuracy of any information.

It might be asked why anyone would consider a retired psychologist with only modest financial security to be an expert on success. "Success," however, is *what we define it to be*, and I have succeeded in accomplishing each of my most important goals. I "absorbed" my mother's assumption that—like her beloved father, a high school principal—I would become well educated, and I met this goal by earning two master's and a doctoral degree. My father felt that he made another man rich by conducting that man's business for fifty years and repeatedly advised me not to work for someone else; I succeeded in heeding that advice by remaining self-employed throughout my career. I wanted a profession that would permit me to help others and my work as a psychologist has led me to feel that many were benefited. I wanted an equal partnership marriage with someone I respect and admire, which I have attained with Sandy. We wanted a loving family with children who would become happy and independent adults, and Ben and Daniel are not only that but also the people whose company we most enjoy. I wanted a group of trusted friends with whom I could relax and "goof off," another goal I have achieved. My body image was troubled by a deformed foot and childhood obesity, but I have successfully compensated by developing an exercise addiction. Finally, it has been my goal to write a book since I first read Steinbeck and Conan Doyle when I was twelve. Although not the great American novel I imagined I would write, this is the second book I have succeeded in publishing.

Like most of us, I would have welcomed greater wealth. I suspect, however, that if that had been one of my top priorities I would not have been as successful at accomplishing my more important goals. Although it is natural that great wealth would be considered the pinnacle of success in our capitalist society, each of us chooses our own definition of success—and not having had more money is almost never what we most regret as we approach the end of life.

Because I am human, I cannot help but experience *pride* about my successes. I do my best, however, to instead remain humble about my many imperfections, considerate of the misfortunes that have afflicted so many, and *grateful* for the good fortune that has permitted my successes. I have been *fortunate* to inherit sufficient potential and to have been born into, and grown up in, an environment that fostered my development and rewarded my efforts. I was most *fortunate* to become connected to someone as talented and thoughtful as Sandy.

I was also *fortunate* to stumble into the *focused positivity* strategy early in my life, as well as to gradually recognize its nature and value—and to now be able to present it as a systematic strategy that anyone might employ to enhance their success and peace of mind. "Gratitude" is a far more appropriate and beneficial attitude than is pride.

1

Introduction

This book has two primary goals:

1. to increase the attainment of goals among those of us who have been impeded by thoughts that undermine our motivation and
2. to enhance peace of mind among those of us who suffer more anxiety or sadness than is justified by healthy concern or normal grieving.

Most of us could benefit from attaining one of these goals; many by attaining both.

OUR ONE SUPERPOWER

Each of us has one true "superpower" to employ in our quest for success and peace of mind: *our ability to shift the focus of our attention*. At any moment in time we can redirect our attention *away* from a thought that provokes excessive pessimism, hesitancy, or distress and *toward* alternatives more likely to inspire optimism and constructive action. Deliberately refocusing our attention in a systematic manner is not only likely to improve our attainment of our goals but also to improve our emotional experience. When we identify reasons to be more hopeful and motivated, we become more likely to take advantage of the opportunities that come our way. A more hopeful view of reality also enhances our peace of mind, an effect that is reinforced and magnified by whatever increase in success we can manage.

We can accomplish more of our goals—and attain greater contentment—by learning to

1. be more mindful of our thoughts,
2. recognize thoughts that are undermining our motivation and hope,
3. generate reasonable alternative ideas that are more likely to reassure or inspire constructive action, and
4. focus as much of our attention as possible on these positive alternatives.

Even in the face of seeming disaster, we can increase our effectiveness and best preserve our peace of mind by redirecting our attention to a less toxic perspective. In addition to increasing our success and peace of mind, this *focused positivity* strategy can be employed to enhance our self-esteem, assertiveness, relationships, relaxation, health-related habits, and connection to the world around us.

PROFESSIONAL ASSISTANCE

Anxiety or depression can become so severe as to rob us of sufficient energy or emotional control to have a reasonable chance of success. In such cases, a neurology-based condition may be present that can only be managed with medications and/or professional treatment. Self-help efforts are not always a reasonable substitute for medical or psychological care. Almost anyone could benefit from the ideas presented in this book, however, and they would most likely serve as a useful treatment adjunct for those of us who receive professional mental health care.

THE BENEFITS OF POSITIVITY

Nearly seventy years ago, Norman Vincent Peale, a Christian minister in Manhattan, wrote *The Power of Positive Thinking*, which became one of the most popular self-help books of all time. His primary message was simple and compelling: We will all be more successful and happier if we think positively. Psychological research has supported this premise. Positive thinking has been shown to enhance creativity, relationships, and even health.

Many of the ideas Peale presents, however, are unrealistic, unscientific, dependent on unconventional religious views, and (most importantly) inaccessible. This book presents a more comprehensive and accessible approach to positive thinking—one that is independent of belief system and consistent with what science has discovered about negativity bias, automatic behavior, the impact of self-talk on mood and behavior, habit change, and even the competition that occurs between the two hemispheres of our brains.

This book is a guide to employing focused positivity to improve our accomplishment of personal goals and enhance that universally prized but elusive goal—peace of mind. By more deliberately focusing our attention, we can increase the positivity of our thinking, increase optimism, diminish anxiety, enhance motivation, inspire more self-assertion, and gradually attain a more balanced view of ourselves and the events of our lives.

UNSPOKEN WORDS THAT DISRUPT
OUR PEACE OF MIND

Sticks and stones can break my bones, but words can never hurt me is an adage we teach our children to insulate them from the cruel remarks of others. As adults, however, words that arise spontaneously from *within*—the self-disparagements, disturbing recollections, and ominous forecasts—cause us emotional pain and prevent us from living our fullest and most productive lives. The human brain has provided us with the technology that has allowed us to dominate the planet but is also the source of many unreasonable feelings of hopelessness and helplessness. Even when we have no good reason to be pessimistic or reluctant, our minds can be spontaneously flooded with disturbing thoughts about ourselves or our circumstances that inhibit actions that would most likely be constructive.

OUR NEGATIVITY BIAS

Many of our failures to act in our own best interests—and much of our unnecessary emotional distress—occur because our attention is automatically drawn to whatever most angers or frightens us, even when there is no emergency. Our motivation and mood, furthermore, tend to be more harmed by each negative thought than improved by each positive one. These two tendencies constitute what researchers call our *negativity bias*, which helps to explain why (1) we sometimes fail to pursue our goals and dreams and (2) we struggle to attain peace of mind—that elusive mental equilibrium in which we accept both ourselves and our circumstances without experiencing distress about something that happened or that might happen in the future.

SELF-TALK AND FUNCTIONAL THINKING

The internal monologue that endlessly streams through our waking consciousness, governing our mood and actions, is called *self-talk*. Thoughts that cause us distress without inspiring constructive action are *dysfunctional*. Dysfunctional thoughts often spring to mind spontaneously, hijack our self-talk, and spoil our motivation and mood. If permitted to linger in the spotlight of our attention, they can inhibit constructive action and disrupt whatever peace of mind we have managed to attain. In contrast, thoughts are *functional* when they reassure, inspire corrective action, or simply provide a more balanced and acceptable view of ourselves and the events of our lives. Focusing on functional thoughts tends to inspire constructive action and enhance peace of mind.

FOCUSING OUR ATTENTION

Our emotional state is often shaped by where we focus our attention. Like all human behavior, our thinking is often *automatic*; it happens without any conscious decision making on our part. Driving a vehicle is probably the most familiar example of an activity we perform "automatically," at least until some unexpected occurrence suddenly jerks our conscious awareness back to the current moment. Although automatic behavior can save us considerable time and energy, dysfunctional thoughts that spontaneously spring into our mind are counterproductive. When the interaction between our biology and our experience has left us cynical about life or hypercritical of ourselves, the thoughts that automatically enter our minds tend to evoke remorse, anger, or fear. Even though dysfunctional reflexive thoughts are usually incomplete, unreasonable, or totally inaccurate, when they are allowed to linger in the spotlight of our attention, the resultant self-talk is likely to undermine both our motivation and our peace of mind.

BECOMING MORE MINDFUL OF OUR THOUGHTS

To change a behavior, we must first recognize it. *Mindfulness* means being aware of whatever is going on in our bodies and minds in the current moment. Although it is commonly used as a meditative technique to enhance relaxation, mindfulness of our thoughts permits us to recognize ideas that are impeding or distressing us unnecessarily. We can then respond by identifying—and focusing on—functional alternatives more conducive to relaxation and constructive action, key ingredients for enhancing peace of mind. We can further improve our motivation, mood, and self-image through review, rehearsal, and role-play of functional self-talk. Focused positivity can also serve as the foundation for our efforts to become more assertive, relaxed, healthier, and more connected to the world around us.

A FIRST SMALL STEP

Attaining greater success and peace of mind, like any change for the better, requires some degree of focused effort and specific action:

1. Begin a *Record of Functional Thought*, a place to list ideas identified as likely to improve motivation and mood. Employ a record-keeping system that fits your established habits. If you are in the habit of keeping notes on a cell phone or e-tablet, use that device. If you use a computer extensively, creating a dedicated file would probably be best. If you are not accustomed to recording information electronically, use a notebook or journal or collection of file cards.

2. Title the first "page" of your *Record* "Gratitude List" and record as many reasons as you can find to be grateful. These should include as many fortunate circumstances or experiences (for example, positive aspects of your birth or childhood, any people who have made a positive contribution to your life better, or positive personal attributes—such as strengths or talents) as possible. Each time you recognize an additional circumstance or person or personal attribute that has benefited your life in some way—or even just a positive event of circumstance somewhere in the world—add it to your list.

3. Review your "Gratitude List" at least one each day and whenever you are feeling sad or anxious and would like to improve your mood.

4. Avoid "doomscrolling," clicking on one outrageous image or tagline after another. When tempted, review your gratitude list instead.

5. When social media content becomes upsetting, consider taking a "break"—or even closing your account altogether—and relying instead on email or phoning to stay in touch with others.

Research has shown that these steps tend to brighten mood and enhance productivity. A sense of gratitude has also been found to act as a buffer against stress and cause us to be more generous and helpful to others—to be more likely to make our world a little bit better place to live.

2

Finding a Better Perspective

When it comes to attaining success and peace of mind, some thoughts are better than others. Some thoughts are *dysfunctional*; they trigger emotional distress—fear, anger, or despondency—without inspiring either constructive action or hope for the future. Examples of these would be:

This will ruin my life.
I'm sure to fail and be humiliated.
I've blown my chance to find love/success/happiness.
I'll never recover from this.

Dysfunctional thoughts such as these can spring into our mind at any time, become the focus of our attention, and disrupt our motivation and peace of mind—even though they are almost always incomplete, unreasonable, or grossly inaccurate. We can improve both our mood and our motivation, therefore, by engaging our conscious awareness to (1) recognize the dysfunctional thought that has caused our distress and (2) search for—and focus our attention on—alternative thoughts that are more balanced, instructive, inspiring, and reassuring. Although we may not be able to control which idea spontaneously comes into ur mind, by becoming mindful of distressing dysfunctional thoughts we can learn to shift our attention to alternatives more likely to inspire constructive action and peace of mind.

Thoughts are *functional* when they inspire self-assertion or reframe the situation as one that does not require action. Although overused, traditional adages typically involve functional thinking, such as:

Time heals all wounds.
This too shall pass.
What doesn't kill me will make me stronger.
Where there's a will, there's a way!

Less hackneyed thoughts that are also functional include:

If I do my best to find a solution, I'll eventually solve (or at least survive) this problem.
This event is probably not as bad as it initially seems and will probably prove to be only a disappointment that I can survive and surmount.
Everything I need to thrive is either within me or within my reach.
Everything that's been damaged or lost can be repaired, replaced, or successfully lived without.

THE EMOTIONAL POWER OF SELF-TALK

Far more than we usually recognize, our thoughts determine how we feel. It often *seems* that our emotional reactions are the direct result of the events and circumstances we encounter. Our feelings, however, are more often a reaction to our "self-talk," the internal monologue that interprets our every experience and observation. Whenever we encounter change, our brains engage in a four-step process that—without our conscious awareness—elicits a feeling state. The process is shown in table 2.1.

Table 2.1.   How the Language of Our Thoughts Arouses Our Emotions

1	→	2	→	3	→	4
We become aware of an external event or circumstance		Thoughts arise spontaneously based on our biology and experience		An internal monologue ("self-talk") takes place		An emotional reaction is triggered

When our emotional reaction is negative, we tend to seek an environmental remedy, some course of action that might mitigate the event or circumstance that prompted our disturbing self-talk. When we are unable to find an acceptable solution, altering our self-talk becomes the most promising means of managing our emotions and preserving our peace of mind.

Our ability to communicate through language is what most clearly distinguishes us from other animals. The ability to express our thoughts in words has permitted us to readily exchange complex information, preserve our discoveries, and pass an ever-expanding body of *collective learning* from one generation to the next. This accumulation of knowledge has led to the rise of cities and nations, the Industrial Revolution, atomic energy (and weapons), the Internet, social media, modern medicine, and the impending era of artificial intelligence. Without language, we would probably still be living as did our foraging ancestors seventy thousand years ago.

Language provides both the structure and the content of our thinking. The words that comprise our internal self-talk—even if never written or spoken aloud—can profoundly affect our feelings about ourselves and the world around us, the decisions we make, the actions we take, and our emotional state. Contrary to the "sticks and stones" adage, words *can* cause us great harm when they inhibit or disturb us and remain in the focus of our attention, unchallenged by more constructive or consoling alternative ideas. It is not surprising, therefore, that consciously identifying—and selectively focusing on—more positive language is a key to enhancing our success and peace of mind.

TRYING TO "SEE" WHAT WE DON'T

Research has shown that our perceptions and beliefs are often inaccurate, even when we feel certain they are perfect. Our minds are subject to many illusions and often play tricks on us. For example, we tend to remember the beginnings and ends of experiences and forget about what happened in between. Our imagination fills in the gaps in our imperfect memories, and we are later unable to distinguish what occurred from what was "imagined." We tend to overlook truthful information that contradicts our beliefs and incorporate information that corroborates them, even if false.

Just as our eyes can be fooled by an illusion or a sleight of hand artist, our minds sometimes misperceive reality. Rather than basing our decisions on a logical analysis of relevant evidence, we often base them on whatever memory is most immediately available. An easily recalled image that is horrifying can make us lose sight of more rational considerations.

Even our basic assumptions about the world can be flawed, as Radiolab cohost Lulu Miller notes in her book *Why Fish Don't Exist*. The book's title refers to the scientific finding that the animals we refer to as "fish" actually belong to several very different families of vertebrates, some of which are more closely related to us than to other animals that use tails and fins to swim.

Research has also shown that when confronted with an unfamiliar problem, the first response that comes to mind—our "gut feeling"—is usually wrong, even though we tend to trust it. The "first instinct fallacy," the mistaken idea that we should trust our immediate instinct, results because our automatic assumptions are often incorrect, even when they feel right. Challenging our spontaneous thoughts with other perspectives, therefore, can help us avoid unnecessary distress and inhibition.

As has been observed by psychologist and author Steven Pinker, we tend to have an unreasonably negative view of the world because bad events usually happen suddenly and make headlines, while positive changes usually occur slowly and incrementally and make poor news copy. Stories about shockingly negative events (for example, the pandemic, rising fascism, looming socialism, incidents of racial injustice, super hurricanes, massive fires, etc.) tend to grab and hold our attention, whereas we tend to be bored by statistics that show gradual improvement in living standards. Although media coverage might make it seem that the world is unraveling—and there will always be short-term downturns and individual catastrophes—there has never been a better time to be alive with respect to life expectancy, infant mortality, violent conflict, food availability, human rights, and standards of living. This is the type of functional thought that we can focus on to feel more grateful and hopeful.

Virtually everything in our lives is *relative* and it is our *perspective* that determines how we feel. Whether we feel rich or poor depends on (1) where we stand with respect to our peers, (2) how our financial status has recently changed, and (3) whether we are comparing ourselves to those who are worse off or better off. Most of us say that we would prefer to make $50,000 per year in a world where everyone else makes $25,000 than make $100,000 in a world where everyone else makes $200,000—even if all costs were the same. Olympians who win bronze medals (third place) are usually more pleased than those who win silver (second place) because they tend to compare themselves to the many contestants who won no medal, whereas second-place finishers tend to compare themselves to the gold medal winner. Our reference point can play a greater role in determining how we feel than reality.

When a thought causes us distress, therefore, it makes perfect sense to consider the possibility that it may be unreasonable, incomplete, or even completely inaccurate. It would serve us to remember that, if we look for them, we can almost always find reasonable alternative thoughts more likely to reassure and inspire.

THE COMPETING PARTS OF OUR MIND

Our brains are divided into two halves ("hemispheres") that are connected but have different relationships to the world. Only our right hemisphere has direct contact with the external world, as it collects the information perceived by our senses, mainly what we see and hear. That data is passed on to the left hemisphere, which uses it to construct a *model* of reality. The left hemisphere then uses this "virtual" world it has constructed to guide our efforts to fulfill our material and organizational needs. The goal of the left brain is to employ our language and physical capacities to secure food, wealth, and property, often by manipulating others in some way. The left hemisphere is acquisitive and competitive and separates people into categories to simplify and control them. Although critical for our survival, the left brain is also responsible for our arrogance, paranoia, and exploitation, and it invents narratives that justify our unreasonable actions.

Our right hemisphere, on the other hand, "sees" the bigger picture. It understands historical and situational context, emotional relationships, moral values, empathy, artistic expression, and feelings that transcend material objects (spirituality, religion, love, etc.). The goal of the right brain is to connect us—and share positive feelings—with others, build a sense of commonality, and appreciate natural and artistic beauty. The right hemisphere cares about people and things other than just ourselves. It sees the ways in which we are similar and united and is responsible for our humility, compassion, and sense of community.

As different as they are, each hemisphere is essential and dependent on the other. Motivation from the left hemisphere ensures that we seek food and shelter—and is even responsible for the scientific research that has provided our understanding of the brain. Right brain motivation, on the other hand, leads us to seek the gratification that comes from enjoying friends, sharing affection with loved ones, and our involvement in community, music, art, literature, and spirituality.

When poet Walt Whitman wrote "I am large, I contain multitudes" (*Song of Myself*, 1855), he was referring to the many contradictions within each of our personalities. Many of our apparent inconsistencies result from the lateralization of our brain, the differences between our left and right hemispheres.

We are almost always subject to competing motivations. Our beliefs and actions are the result of a counterbalance, a push and pull of competing aspects of our mind, some conscious, some unconscious. Once we reach a conclusion, however, we tend to quickly forget the competing alternatives and develop unfounded confidence in the option we have selected. When that view causes distress, however, it is entirely reasonable that we consider alternatives that would be more inspirational or comforting.

Our emotional distress tends to result from thoughts that originate in the left hemisphere. Functional alternatives, on the other hand, are often products of the right hemisphere. A peculiar experience has been found to occur when the left hemisphere of our brain shuts down (for example, due to injury, illness, or anesthesia) but the right hemisphere remains functional. Despite the complete loss of verbal communication that occurs during left brain incapacity, when affected individuals regain their left brain function, they tend to express regret about having lost what they report was an extremely pleasant reverie. Although left brain function is critical to survival, our peace of mind is more likely to be enhanced by focusing on thoughts inspired by the right hemisphere, including those related to our appreciation of others, nature, and the arts.

Both the virtual model created by our left hemisphere and the automatic thoughts it produces are far from complete and often inaccurate. The left hemisphere is often "blind" to more functional perspectives of our right hemisphere. Though relegated to secondary status because it is "silent," our right hemisphere is often our best source of functional thought.

FOCUSING ON WHAT MATTERS MOST

Few of us are in the habit of searching for alternative perspectives. On the contrary, our *confirmation bias* causes us to automatically scan for evidence that supports the perspective we already hold—even when incorrect and unreasonably disturbing. Furthermore, our *introspection illusion*—the incorrect assumption that we understand the origins of our mental states—causes us to mistakenly think that our views are the result of careful reasoning rather than irrational bias. By learning to be more mindful and making a deliberate effort, however, we can find alternative viewpoints that are both reasonable and more positive.

Thoughts are functional to the extent that they

1. diminish the importance we attribute to whatever has been lost or damaged,
2. reduce the extent of anticipated damage,
3. diminish our sense of responsibility for having caused the damage or loss, or
4. make the loss or damage seem more reparable or tolerable.

Devaluing what we have lost or never been able to obtain is a strategy that we have used to mitigate disappointment since we first acquired language. Although the moral that Aesop intended for his "The Fox and the Grapes" fable was that "it's easy to despise what we can't have," reframing as less desirable those things that we are unable to obtain ("sour grapes thinking") does no harm, eases distress, and enhances peace of mind. In other words, it is *functional*.

Psychologist Fritz Perls suggested that when we become very distressed as the result of an event that most of us would consider "minor" (for example, the outcome of a game, another driver acting rudely, being socially snubbed, etc.), we surrender our peace of mind for "chicken shit." He further noted that when we experience great distress in reaction to a more significant event—but one that falls short of genuine tragedy—we surrender our peace of mind for "elephant shit." His point was that most of the things we allow to upset us are just "shit," and we would all be better off if we refused to allow "shit" to rule our emotional lives.

Examples of thoughts that are functional because they *diminish the importance* of what we have lost or that has been damaged include:

All that's been lost is money, time, or a material object—nothing that's truly precious or irreplaceable.

So long as the people I care about are okay, this loss doesn't matter so much.

All I really need to be fulfilled is love and basic security—nothing else is essential.

Examples of thoughts that are functional because they *diminish the degree of harm* we expect to result from an unwanted event or circumstance include:

As upsetting as this is, I'll find some way to survive, cope, and carry on.

Shit happens and life goes on.

Examples of thoughts that are functional because they tend to diminish *the degree of our responsibility* for whatever harm results include:

Life is complicated and I'm only human; what I did seemed to be for the best at the time.

Taking everything I didn't know or understand into consideration, I did as well as could reasonably be expected.

My role in producing this outcome was probably far less important than I think.

Examples of thoughts that are functional because they *make the damage or loss seem more reparable or tolerable* include:

What seems overwhelming to me today is likely to appear far less disturbing tomorrow and probably even less consequential in the distant future.

No misfortune, no matter how great, means that I'll be miserable forever.

Although my attention is naturally drawn to what I've lost, every crisis also creates opportunities—and maybe even a path to a better future.

I can do this; I'll figure it out.

THOUGHTS MATTER
EVEN IN THE WORST OF TIMES

Although a positive outlook generally improves our chances for success and peace of mind, in some instances it can be healthiest for us to—at least temporarily—allow ourselves to be miserable. When we have lost a close loved one, it can be impossible to experience anything but grief. During such moments—which can occur long after a major loss—attempting to think more positively can seem disrespectful to both the deceased and the magnitude of the loss. When we are appropriately miserable, we are more likely to benefit from commiseration and validation of our distress than we would from any "positive spin."

No matter how devastated we may have been by our loss, however, at some point in the bereavement process our recovery is likely to be helped by functional thoughts such as:

I have reasons to go on—people who value me and want me to survive, opportunities to contribute to my family or community, worthwhile causes to which I can contribute.

Others have survived and recovered from similar losses, and they may be available to help me find a way through this.

I've overcome all the challenges and obstacles life has thrown in my path so far; I'll find a way through this one too.

Tragedies like this represent misfortune, not punishment or lack of personal merit.

I can survive any loss if I decide to take each moment one at a time and just do what seems to be the next right thing.

FEW LOSSES ARE TOTAL

Whenever we can identify a potential benefit of an unwanted event, we reframe it as a partial "cost" of something desirable and it becomes easier to live with. For example, research has shown that when PTSD sufferers learn that dreaming about a traumatic experience *decreases* the intensity of emotional reactions to reminders of the trauma, their *traumatic nightmares* become less distressing. In other words, reinterpreting disturbing dreams as a step toward recovery diminishes the distress they provoke.

Some thoughts are functional because they call our attention to unrecognized *positive consequences* ("silver linings") that accompany almost every unwanted event, such as:

I can learn more from this "failure" than I'd ever be likely to learn from a success.

The best part of life may be the deep satisfaction that comes from surviving a struggle.

Both the great advances in human civilization and the heroic actions of individuals have occurred because great duress demanded inspired action.

Things go wrong so that we can appreciate them when they go right.

Although this seems like a disaster right now, it may prepare me to better cope with what will come later.

ALLAYING OUR PERSONAL FEARS

Our personal fears—of failure, embarrassment, displeasing someone, etc.—can prevent us from assertively pursuing our goals. When anxiety threatens to impede us from taking what seems to be reasonable action, therefore, we may be helped by focusing our attention on a functional idea, such as:

> Failure can't define me if I refuse to permit it.
> The more familiar I become with what I fear, the less it can control me.
> My mistakes and failings demonstrate that I'm challenging myself and taking the risks necessary to succeed.
> I'll be able to straighten out, overcome, and survive any honest mistake.

THOUGHTS THAT ARE FUNCTIONAL FOR SPECIFIC SITUATIONS

Many of the thoughts that most comfort us are situational, specific to the self-talk that in the moment has elicited our distress. Although we are similar in many ways, we can interpret events very differently. Adages and homilies are often less effective at mitigating our distress than language tailored specifically to our immediate circumstances. For example, the distress associated with *losing a job* is likely to be eased by considering thoughts such as:

> Now I'll have the time I've been wanting to spend with the kids/take care of my declining parents/etc.
> This may be the opportunity I've been wanting to fulfill my dream of starting a business/completing my education/writing my book/ getting into shape, etc.

At last, I've escaped the grind of performing this job that I never liked.

Thank goodness I'll never again have to deal with that supervisor/coworker who treated me so poorly.

During a pandemic such as that which struck globally in 2020, it can be comforting to focus our attention on functional thoughts such as:

Taking precautions can ensure that I'll survive this crisis.

An experience like this can clarify what's most important and even lead me to dedicate myself to higher values, such as demonstrating how much I care about my loved ones.

This tragic event may increase recognition of the importance of international cooperation so that the world will be better prepared for something similar in the future.

This reminds us that nothing is guaranteed and that we should make the most of every day and act on our dreams while we're able.

Even after the pandemic passes, more people will be working from home, easing traffic congestion and the urban housing shortage and benefiting the environment.

This won't go on forever; life will become more "normal" after a reliable vaccine becomes available.

We have been lucky that this virus has not had a higher fatality rate or severely affected many children.

When we are "brokenhearted" because a romantic partner has left—or behaved so badly that we have no reasonable choice but to end the relationship—it can help to entertain functional thoughts such as:

Thank goodness I found out who they are now rather than later.

I'm far better off single and on my own than with someone who doesn't appreciate me.

A list of my ex's negatives would be long and would include . . .

Now I have the freedom and opportunity to build a rewarding independent life (and to prepare myself for a new relationship if I
decide to pursue another).

As many have proven, it is possible to construct a wonderful life
without a marriage-like relationship.

When we are not offered a coveted job, we may be able to avoid a
crisis of self-doubt by considering functional thoughts such as:

If these people don't appreciate or want me, this clearly isn't the right
employer for me.

Those interviewers seemed like they would have been difficult to
work for, so it's probably for the best that I won't be working there.

Now I can cross that company off my list of potential employers and
move forward toward connecting with one who will appreciate
what I have to offer.

The experience I gained from this process will help me deal better
with future interviews by prospective employers.

When a disliked candidate wins the big election, our disappointment
may be mitigated if we focus on thoughts that compete with the notion
of a true disaster, such as:

As much as I dislike the winner, some of his or her policies will probably benefit me or someone I care about.

At least Uncle Kevin will be happy.

Politics goes through cycles, and this is most likely just an extreme
swing that will be followed by a correction.

All progress involves setbacks; my fear of losing everything that's
been accomplished is almost certainly based on illusion.

This adversity may be exactly what's needed to generate the motivation and energy that will get us back on track.

When another driver acts unreasonably and prevents us from getting through an intersection before the light turns red, our frustration can be mitigated if we can find a storyline that includes a positive aspect to the event, such as:

If I'd made that light, I might have been at an intersection ahead at the wrong time and been plowed into by an impaired driver running a red light.

Maybe this is how the universe reminds me to slow down, relax more, and accept more peacefully whatever comes my way.

This may be my opportunity to demonstrate how an enlightened and mature driver skillfully avoids—and then graciously forgives— a troubled driver.

When a favorite team loses the big game, our frustration can be diminished if we can identify and focus on thoughts that call attention to either how someone with whom we identify may have benefited or on the relative meaninglessness of the whole endeavor:

It's been so long since that city won any kind of championship that it's only right that their team won this one.

Somewhere in that team's city there's someone much like me who's been cheered up by this result.

Some players on my team seem inconsiderate/arrogant/less than fully committed/etc., so maybe this loss will serve as a needed wakeup call.

In the grand scheme of life, sports contests have little or no real significance for nonparticipants.

As the only part of my team that's preserved from year to year is the uniform, I'm essentially rooting for "laundry" (*Seinfeld* TV show).

Those among us who have become very distressed about growing older may be comforted by functional thoughts such as:

I'll probably feel less stressed and happier in retirement; most people do.

By finding the affection and balance that is most often attained in later life, I can make the years to come the most fulfilling.

I'll find opportunities to learn and grow once I'm off the treadmill of work and/or raising a family.

Even anxieties provoked by thoughts of our own death can be soothed by paying greater attention to functional ideas such as:

By clearly demonstrating my love for the people who are important to me, I'll be better prepared to accept dying.

Death is just a natural and inevitable part of life.

Death brings complete peace, with no stress, worry, anger, sorrow, pain, debt, or risk.

COPING WITH REJECTION

Most of us find it emotionally painful to be rejected, disliked, or not accepted. These experiences upset us by provoking dysfunctional thoughts, such as:

This must mean that there is something wrong with me, that I'm lacking in some way.

I won't be able to stand it unless everyone likes, or at least accepts, me.

We are also likely to become distressed when someone expresses a viewpoint with which we strongly disagree—and even more distressed when our efforts to present a different point of view result in even more adamant expression of the opinion we abhor. Experiences of this type can also elicit dysfunctional thoughts, such as:

This person must be disturbed or stupid (or even "evil") to hold such a horrible opinion.

As my attempt to "correct" the unreasonable opinion only escalated our conflict, reconciliation is hopeless.

In circumstances of this type, our peace of mind may depend on our ability to remember—and focus our attention on—more functional thoughts, such as:

The beliefs and actions of others are not so much a response to who I am as they are a result of how their minds have been "programmed" to respond (a fact that the major social media platforms have utilized to acquire vast fortunes).

We all tend to pay greatest attention to information that corroborates and strengthens our biases, to discount information that contradicts them, and to devalue sources of contradictory information.

The more we know about someone, the easier it is to understand their beliefs and actions, no matter how unreasonable they might seem.

If I had shared all the experiences of that person, I'd probably believe and behave similarly.

If I understood everything that has led this person to their opinions, I'd have more empathy, I might be able to stop promoting my viewpoint, and I would be able to respond in a way that would bring us closer together (rather than driving us apart).

When we attempt to change someone's opinion, we tend to push that person away, improve their ability to justify the opinion they hold, and become perceived as someone whose opinion can't be trusted.

Instead of belittling or attacking another's point of view, I'm more likely to have a positive impact by attempting to understand how they came to hold that opinion and sharing some of the experiences that led me to hold my opinion.

Neither my health nor my prosperity depend on that person changing his or her perspective.

THOUGHTS THAT ARE FUNCTIONAL BECAUSE THEY SYNC WITH OUR BELIEFS

Some thoughts are functional because they harmonize with the tenets
of our religious faith or philosophical viewpoint. In the face of great
adversity, those who believe in the existence of a *divine plan*—in which
a Supreme Being controls all human experience in the service of an
ultimate purpose—may be comforted by thoughts such as:

As this too has been ordained by God, it must be for the best in some
way that is beyond my understanding.
Acts of repentance and devotion will secure my absolution, connection with God, and eternal peace.
God (for Christians, Muslims, and Jews) or karma (for Buddhists
and Hindus) will ensure that all debts and injustices are eventually
repaid and resolved.
God (or karma) will provide either the means to succeed or trials that
will make me stronger.
Although the past is history and the future a mystery, the "present"
is a gift from God that gives me power to influence my experience
of life.

Even when genuine tragedy strikes in the form of the death of a
loved one, religious faith may permit us to take comfort in functional
thoughts such as:

Although this loss is agonizing for me because I must continue to live
without my deceased loved one, my loved one has been relieved
of all pain—physical and emotional—and is now experiencing
eternal peace.

My loved one is now with God in heaven, where there is no fear, tension, conflict, worry, or frustration.

My loved one lives on in the spiritual world and is destined to be born again.

I'll be reunited with my loved one in the afterlife.

I can try to live the best life possible in dedication to the memory of my loved one.

A structured philosophy of life, like a religious faith, can generate ideas that help us preserve our peace of mind in times of duress. *Stoicism*, an ancient philosophy that places honorable behavior above all else, encourages consideration of functional thoughts such as:

Knowing that life is short and that we all will die can help me remember to "seize the day" and make the most of my limited time on Earth.

Encountering difficulties teaches me that I can survive almost anything, overcome adversity, and become stronger in the process.

Every "problem" I encounter gives me the opportunity to turn it "upside down" into something good.

Life is much like a tennis serve; I have no control over how the ball comes at me, but all that matters is how I hit it back.

As much philosophy as religion, *Buddhism* emphasizes the seeking of enlightenment through meditation and respect for all forms of life. Buddhism encourages consideration of functional thoughts such as:

I can enhance my peace of mind by rejecting my primitive desires for the world to be different than it is.

Approaching others with honesty and respect, and ignoring my urges to control events or people, will bring me closer to enlightenment and absolute peace than will getting what I crave.

The most important goal of social interaction is removing barriers
between people, not making a good impression or obtaining some
desired material object.

Determinism is another system of philosophical belief that can generate many functional thoughts but that may be difficult for many of
us to accept because it denies the existence of *free will*. Those of us
who are determinists believe that our actions are entirely the result of
an interaction between the biology we inherit and the impact of our
environmental exposure—neither of which are under our control. Although this belief is consistent with the neuroscientific evidence, it is
inconsistent with the tenets of most religions and many personal belief
systems. For those who can accept it, deterministic philosophy offers
many functional perspectives, such as:

As human actions are entirely determined by factors outside our
conscious control, all mistakes and bad acts—either by me or by
others—are inevitable, understandable, and forgivable.

When it seems that I have done harm, my best course of action is
to apologize to anyone I've offended, offer to make amends, and
prepare myself to do better in the future—sacrificing as little peace
of mind as possible to guilt or shame.

By recognizing that the behavior that offended me resulted from the
programming of the offender's brain, I may be able to substitute
pity and concern for rage and use forgiveness to best preserve my
peace of mind.

By learning to be more accepting of what I can't change and influence what I can for the better, I may be able to *nudge* the future in
the direction I would like to see it go.

NO MORE WORK THAN WE CAN MANAGE

Although recognizing dysfunctional thoughts and refocusing our attention toward more functional alternatives can enhance our success and

peace of mind, just *wishing* we were in that habit is unlikely to change anything. There are no miracle transformations, only methods that can be effective *when consistently practiced.*

Specific steps to reverse a habit of focusing on dysfunctional thoughts are presented here. They involve summoning the conscious awareness and energy to

1. recognize automatic thoughts that have resulted in a negative emotional state (for example, shame, guilt, anger, fear, despondency, etc.),
2. identify as many alternative thoughts as possible that are both reasonable and functional, and
3. focus as much attention as possible on those functional thoughts.

Acquiring this behavior pattern requires substantial—but not unreasonable—amounts of time and effort. Consistently employing these steps is likely to both inspire constructive self-assertion and improve our emotional experience.

1. Whenever an event or circumstance leads to emotional distress, attempt to identify and record the automatic dysfunctional thought or thoughts that prompted your distress. Because it is best to focus as little attention as possible on dysfunctional thoughts, they should be recorded in a separate file or on a back page of the *Record of Functional Thought* you started at the end of chapter 1—where they won't be encountered each time you open it.
2. On the next "page" of your *Record* immediately after your "Gratitude List," record your responses to the following questions about each event or circumstance that has led to distress:
   a. If all the things I care about in life add up to 100 percent, what percentage is likely to remain intact *despite* this event or circumstance?
   b. How likely is it that I'll be able to overcome or successfully survive this event?

    c. In what ways might this event prove to be of benefit to—or inspire constructive action by—me or someone I care about?

3. List as many other functional alternative thoughts as you can identify in your *Record*, borrowing or modifying any examples from this chapter that may be appropriate.
4. Review your *Record* with one or more trusted others (for example, close friend, sibling, mentor, therapist, spouse, etc.) and use their input to make modifications and add additional functional thoughts.
5. Keep your *Record* close at hand and review it at least once each day, especially when distressed.
6. Review and revise your *Record* whenever a life event leads to inhibition or emotional distress, repeating steps 1 through 4.

If your progress seems too slow,

1. make an audio recording of your *Record* and listen to it once or more each day,
2. recite your *Record* in front of a mirror once or more each day, or
3. read your *Record* to another trusted other, making alterations and additions based on their feedback.

Systematically focusing on thoughts that reassure and inspire us can help us reshape our perception of reality. The more mindful we become of dysfunctional thoughts and the more we refocus our attention toward functional alternatives, the more our peace of mind is likely to be enhanced.

3

Managing Self-Criticism

Although we hear more of the damage done by the prejudices one group of people holds toward another, as individuals we are often harmed most by our biases against ourselves. Unfortunate experiences during childhood can leave us with an internal spring of self-critical thoughts that, even when unreasonable or entirely inaccurate, infiltrate our self-talk, disrupt our peace of mind, and inhibit potentially constructive action.

WHEN SELF-CRITICISM BECOMES DYSFUNCTIONAL

Some self-criticisms serve a purpose and are, therefore, functional—but only when they are specific (for example, "I could do that better") rather than general (for example, "I screw up everything") and accompanied by an accessible path to improved performance (for example, "I'll get Frank to show me how to do that"). When our personal worth is slighted and no reasonable means of correction can be identified, however, self-criticism is *dysfunctional*; it harms our mood and self-esteem without any compensating benefit.

Like dysfunctional thoughts in general, self-disparaging ideas are typically incomplete and unreasonable and sometimes grossly inaccurate. We can, therefore, improve our mood and motivation using the same focused positivity strategy presented earlier to mitigate the harm done by dysfunctional thoughts about life events. We can inspire assertive action and enhance our peace of mind by learning to

1. be mindful of our thoughts so that we recognize dysfunctional self-criticisms when they arise,
2. respond by identifying as many functional alternative thoughts as possible, and
3. focus as much of our attention as possible on the functional alternatives.

By building this pattern into a habit, we can both enhance our peace of mind and gradually shape a more balanced self-image.

In an ideal world, each of us would devote our energy and personal resources to pursuing our dreams, expressing affection for those we care about, and attaining the most meaningful life experience possible. In the world as it is, however, our efforts are often diverted because we focus excessive attention on reflexive doubts about our abilities or worthiness. Each time we observe ourselves failing to act in our own best interests, furthermore, our self-prejudice is confirmed. In extreme cases this pattern can result in immobilizing levels of performance anxiety, evoke persistent anger at ourselves, and generally cast our life experiences in a negative light. It is not surprising, therefore, that unreasonable levels of self-criticism are associated with both underachievement and depression.

THE ORIGINS OF SELF-PREJUDICE

None of us deserves to feel ashamed for simply being who we are; yet many of us do. We are each born with a unique set of biology-determined strengths and weaknesses and into an overwhelmingly complex and unpredictable world. Furthermore, we have no control over either our genetic inheritance or our early life experience. And it is during childhood, when we are almost completely at the mercy of our environment, that the foundations of our self-image are formed. Through no fault of our own, many of us are exposed to levels of childhood stress or trauma sufficiently intense to create self-prejudice, impede our attainment of adult life goals, and predispose us to anxiety and depression.

Our experience while growing up, especially how we are treated by our primary caretakers, determines most of our early beliefs about ourselves. As children, we attempt to make sense of the circumstances in which we find ourselves, whatever they might be. If we are abused or neglected, therefore, we may reason that we must "deserve" no better and our self-esteem is damaged accordingly. Being repeatedly exposed to the idea that we are deficient in some way can so firmly entrench that thought in our subconscious that it automatically springs to mind whenever we are confronted with a challenge.

Spontaneous messages of self-disparagement (for example, "I'm a loser" or "I can't do anything right") or helplessness (for example, "No one cares about what happens to me" or "Nothing I could do would make any difference") cause us to anticipate failure and destroy our incentive to invest energy and resources in pursuing goals that seem unreachable. Dysfunctional self-doubt can cause us to avoid even reasonable risks, withhold honest self-expression, hide healthy levels of emotional vulnerability, and even tolerate abusive treatment—all of which, of course, further reinforce our self-prejudice.

LIFE ISN'T FAIR

Although the Declaration of Independence suggests that "all men are created equal," the many ways in which we are not equal are obvious. Some of us are faster, stronger, more attractive, more even tempered, unusually talented, better able to focus attention, better at making others laugh, etc. Although advantages like these can help us cope and feel better about ourselves, whether we have them or not is *mostly a matter of luck*—the result of the interaction between our genetic inheritance and the impact of the environment in which we happen to be born and raised.

We have little control over the events and circumstances of our childhood, when our attitudes and personality are formed. Furthermore, life does not provide us with a "level playing field" or equal opportunity for all. Some of us are *fortunate* to have (1) inherited the potential to develop useful attributes and qualities, (2) grown up in an environment that nurtured that potential, and (3) lived in a society that rewards the strengths and talents we happen to possess. Many of us, however, have been born without exceptional potential or into adverse circumstances that either inhibited the development of our potential or failed to reward our particular set of abilities. Once we have matured enough to better understand our circumstances and relationships, however, we can begin to collect "tools" that can provide us with influence over both. Although a greater challenge for those of us who have been unfortunate, *as adults each of us can learn how to find both sufficient motivation and effective strategies for improving the outcomes of our endeavors and enhancing our peace of mind.*

REPROGRAMMING PREJUDICIAL SELF-TALK

Our capacity to manage prejudice has been demonstrated by the many of us who have overcome our inherent aversion to people who *look different* from those with whom we grew up. Because of the survival advantage it provided to our prehistoric ancestors, evolution has left us with an instinctive suspicion of anyone who does not look like the members of our familiar "tribe." In the ancient world an encounter with someone of a different group was often dangerous. Given the diverse communities in which many of us live today, however, this reflexive antipathy can be counterproductive. Many of us compensate, therefore, by rejecting our automatic prejudice and *choosing instead* to focus on thoughts of inclusion, tolerance, and mutual respect. In the same way that we can overcome automatic bias against others, we can also *choose* to reject unreasonable criticisms of ourselves.

Although we cannot prevent our brains from generating thoughts according to how they have been programmed, when those thoughts are counterproductive we can intervene by employing our higher cognitive faculties to generate—and focus on—functional alternatives. By identifying—and focusing on—more inspiring and reassuring ideas, we can enhance our motivation, self-assertion, and peace of mind.

ADOPTING A MORE MATURE PERSPECTIVE

From the perspective of a child, whatever happens can seem our responsibility and elicit unreasonable feelings of guilt and shame. Although logically flawed, this type of childish viewpoint often persists into our adulthood, predisposing us to dysfunctional thinking. For example, we often harbor irrational and dysfunctional suspicions that we could have rectified our parents' problems if only we had been or behaved differently as children. When our self-talk features language such as "If only I'd been better behaved (or more attractive, smarter, talented, etc.), my parents wouldn't have divorced (or been depressed, abused alcohol or drugs, mistreated me, abandoned us, etc.)," negative emotional reactions are elicited that can undermine our motivation and mood.

As adults, we can pursue a more mature viewpoint by shifting our attention to reasonable functional ideas, such as:

No child is ever responsible for the bad acts of an adult.
It's the duty of parents to protect the physical and emotional well-being of their children.
Like all children, I acted as seemed best at the time to my naive and immature mind.

Although they may be blamed for their parents' actions, children are never responsible for them.

Rather than deserving blame or shame, I deserve understanding and compassion for having experienced childhood difficulties.

FUNCTIONAL THOUGHTS ABOUT OURSELVES

Some thoughts about ourselves are functional because they reflect positively on the worth of every person, such as:

Everyone, including me, deserves to be treated with decency and respect.

I have an absolute right to think as I do, express what I think, and pursue what makes me happy.

My survival—despite all the adversity life has thrown in my path—is testimony to my resilience.

The efforts I've made to improve myself and help others merit recognition and approval.

Success or failure is less meaningful than "sincere positive effort," as only the latter is within my control.

Like all humans, I have hidden strengths, untapped potential, and the ability to grow and change in profound ways.

My best efforts sometimes turn out poorly because life is unpredictable and I have normal human limitations.

There's no shame in having been treated badly by life; that's entirely a matter of unfortunate heredity, experience, and opportunity.

Some ideas are functional because they distance us from the unreasonable actions of others:

What other people think and do is *not my business* because they are outside my control.

Offensive words and acts by others define them, not me.

TAMING DYSFUNCTIONAL FEAR

We have only a few *natural* fears—of falling, loud noises, major injury, and strangers. Our other fears are learned, either from observation, adverse experience, or something we have read or been told—and they are often unjustified. One common dysfunctional fear is of the emotional pain we might experience if our self-prejudice is confirmed by a "failure." We can sometimes become so fearful of displaying weakness or fault that we lose our tolerance for any imperfection, making it difficult to form any close interpersonal relationship.

We rely on the fear/rage response to spur us into self-protective action when we are under threat of physical harm. But when the threat is only to our ego and a poor outcome would not be irreparable or intolerable, any fear that inhibits us from attempting constructive action or responsible self-assertion is dysfunctional. When we find ourselves inhibited about taking what seem to be entirely reasonable actions, it may be time to search for prejudicial content in our self-talk and functional alternative thoughts to focus on.

Intense feelings of self-doubt or self-directed anger are often a signal that dysfunctional fear is attempting to hijack the narrative of our self-talk. Once we have determined that our physical integrity is not threatened and that our reluctance is based on fear of the emotional pain that might be caused by a "failure," the goal is to confront the fear directly and honestly—to acknowledge it, own it, and identify response options. Being "brave" does not mean having no fear. It means finding the courage to set aside dysfunctional fears and take reasonable risks, to make sure that we are not confined by irrational and self-imposed limitations.

Stanford psychologist David Burns startles the psychotherapists he trains by presenting them with thirty-six cognitive therapy techniques and advising that their job is to "fail as fast as possible." He quickly clarifies that each patient is likely to benefit from only a few of the techniques and that the therapist's job is to quickly eliminate those that do not work so they can progress to the ones that will work. The functional perspective is to view failure as just a step on the path to eventual success, not a reason to give up or feel ashamed.

Examples of dysfunctional thoughts about failure that might inhibit our best effort include:

Failure would prove that I'm a worthless loser.

I'm too weak to survive another failure.

I can't make a mistake because that would prove I'm incompetent, a failure.

I won't be able to stand it if what I do isn't perfect—or at least the best.

If I don't succeed at this one, it'll mean that I'm unfit for any relationship.

If people learn I made a mistake, they'll lose all respect for me.

Functional alternatives would include thoughts such as:

Life is hard and mistakes are inevitable. I deserve credit for not giving up and persisting.

Like everyone, I sometimes screw up. That makes me human, not a loser.

Every step that allows me to move forward is a "success"—no matter how disappointing its immediate outcome might seem.

Anyone who isn't failing now and then isn't experimenting enough.

Anyone who respects the feelings of others is deserving of respect.

Displaying my integrity and compassion is far more critical to being successful in my personal relationships than is never making a mistake.

Acknowledging—and laughing at—my imperfections and mistakes is likely to trigger empathy and improve my connections with others.

If I continue to do what seems the next right thing, someone will eventually understand and appreciate me.

My experience of fear is normal and understandable, but it can't define me if I refuse to let it prevent me from pursuing my goals and doing what I believe to be right.

No one can always excel, and everyone who makes mistakes is still of value.

There are no "failures," only discoveries.

REFRAMING TRAUMA

For more than sixty years, behavior therapists have been promoting gradual exposure ("desensitization training") as a treatment for anxiety and phobic disorders. Exposure therapies work because they force us to alter our thinking. When we observe ourselves being close to something we dread without being harmed or overwhelmed, we are forced to think "This must not be that dangerous" or "I must not be as fearful as I thought." This same type of cognitive reframing can be used to alter other dysfunctional emotional reactions.

Traumatic childhood events (referred to by psychiatric researchers as adverse childhood experiences or ACEs) are common and their consequences often reach far into adulthood. ACEs include episodes of abuse, humiliation, and prolonged neglect but can also consist of simply witnessing violent or self-destructive behavior. And ACEs often lead to adult problems with anxiety, anger, and unreasonable self-criticism.

One strategy for addressing the adverse effects of childhood trauma involves asking the client to identify ways in which their traumatic experience may have been *to their advantage*. For example, an adult with self-esteem issues related to childhood abuse might be encouraged to review functional thoughts such as:

My personal history has made me more sensitive to the feelings of others—especially other trauma survivors.

As disturbing as my childhood experience was, it has allowed me to see that trauma can be survived—and might even be used as inspiration to create, connect, contribute, and succeed.

My experience has provided me with a realistic view of just how harsh life can sometimes be.

Traumatic experience can alter our view of both ourselves and the world in which we live. Trauma survivors frequently experience spontaneous dysfunctional thoughts, such as:

I caused [the traumatic event] to happen; it was my fault.

If only I had . . . , [the traumatic event] would never have occurred.

I must have deserved what happened to me.

I'll never be able to feel safe again.

No one will ever want to be with me after I've been so traumatized and humiliated.

Although completely normal, these thoughts are at best unreasonable and incomplete and at worst entirely inaccurate. Nevertheless, just as infection can prevent our bodies from healing, preoccupation with such dysfunctional thoughts can disrupt our mind's natural capacity for emotional recovery. By becoming more mindful of our thoughts and developing the habit of shifting our focus away from dysfunctional thoughts to functional alternatives, we can create a more balanced perspective likely to facilitate mental and emotional healing.

This strategy is the cornerstone of *cognitive processing therapy* (CPT), an effective approach to the treatment of posttraumatic stress disorder (PTSD) that has been pioneered by the Veteran's Administration. Over a series of ten to twelve CPT sessions, the therapist helps the PTSD sufferer

1. identify the dysfunctional thoughts that have become the focus of their attention and that are blocking recovery,

2. construct more reasonable, balanced, and functional alternatives, and
3. systematically replace the former with the latter.

When traumatic experience has left us with recurrent dysfunctional thoughts, our recovery can be facilitated by focusing on functional alternative ideas that are more reasonable and balanced, such as:

I'm only human. Given the circumstances of my trauma, I couldn't have acted differently without risking even greater injury. I deserve understanding from others and myself, not criticism.

The traumatic experience happened because I had the misfortune of being in the wrong place at the wrong time.

My heightened feeling of being in danger is a completely normal and understandable—but temporary—reaction to the trauma I survived. If I persist at recovery efforts, my fear will gradually evolve into feelings that are more reasonable and easier to live with.

Having been subjected to trauma has nothing to do with my personal competence or worth.

By rejecting unrealistic fears and gradually taking on reasonable risks, I'll eventually regain my sense of confidence and my full range of self-assertion.

I'm better off apart from anyone who would be so unreasonable as to think less of me because I had the misfortune of being traumatized.

SEEING THROUGH OUR ILLUSIONS

Our self-prejudices are often strengthened by illusions of thought. Our memories and beliefs, like our perceptions, can be subject to distortions that magnify our self-criticism. Our self-image can be improved, however, by learning to recognize the illusions that undermine our

self-confidence or our sense of well-being and respond to them by finding, and focusing on, a more functional alternative viewpoint.

Each of us misunderstands some aspects of reality. Freud observed
that we need illusions to avoid being overwhelmed by the harsh realities
of life. Even the most celebrated "experts" are frequently proved wrong,
and intelligent people can easily be victimized by a sophisticated con
artist. When we make a mistake or get taken advantage of, it can help
to remember that

1. we are all vulnerable to illusion,
2. making a mistake or being taken advantage of doesn't mean that
   we lack ability or are deficient in some way, and
3. every decision we make and every action we take seems at that
   moment to be for the best.

Although it may appear that we should have known better and behaved
differently, this is an illusion created by a retrospective vantage. Even
a moment later, we can no longer recall all the factors that motivated
us to act as we did. The most reasonable way to address disturbing
thoughts about past actions that led to unwanted outcomes, therefore,
is to focus on a functional thought, such as:

I'm only human, and like all humans I'm bound to often get it
   wrong.
Forgiveness is always a reasonable mercy, for myself as well as for
   others.

THE ILLUSION OF PERSONAL
STRENGTH OR WEAKNESS

Many of us believe that we lack some personal quality or trait that is
responsible for the "willpower" or "self-discipline" we admire or envy
in others. But the idea that we are born "with or without" personal

strengths of this type has been disproven many times. Many people who had displayed few signs of self-discipline, and believed they had none, have been able to learn strategies that permit them to act in ways that *appear* to display great willpower. In other words, "willpower" is often an *illusion* that a person has learned to create.

When we observe another person behaving better than we expect we would, we tend to attribute a positive trait (for example, self-discipline, patience, kindness, etc.) to that person and to think that we are lacking in the quality. Scientific research has shown, however, that admirable "characteristics" are often learned rather than inbred. Although it can require some time and attention to find a successful strategy, each of us is capable of learning to display the admirable behaviors we value in others. And when we do, we are likely to gain greater respect not only from others but from ourselves as well.

THE FORCES THAT CONTROL OUR ACTIONS

Our behavior is often determined by an interaction between obstacles and incentives, a balance between all the factors that deter us ("friction") and the combined short-term rewards ("payoff"). Reluctance to engage in an activity we know to be of long-term benefit (for example, exercise, saving, personal organization, tax preparation, etc.) doesn't prove a lack of willpower, it only proves that *we haven't yet found a successful engagement strategy.* There are no supermen or superwomen, only humans who have discovered, or learned how to attain, a balance of motivational factors that supports the performance of a difficult, but valued, activity. The rest of us can learn to create a similar illusion by reducing the friction and increasing the payoff until the scales of our motivational balance are tipped in favor of the constructive activity. When we experience the illusion that we are undisciplined, therefore, it can help to focus on functional alternative thoughts, such as:

My apparent lack of discipline or willpower means only that I haven't yet learned a successful strategy, not that I'm defective.

I can create an illusion of "willpower" by making it easier, more pleasurable, or more rewarding to engage in valued, but previously avoided, behavior.

Strategies that can be employed to create the illusion of willpower are discussed further in the chapter 7 section on acquiring healthier habits.

MORE FUNCTIONAL THOUGHTS THAT MATCH OUR BELIEFS

As is true of thoughts about life events, some ideas about ourselves are functional and useful because they are consistent with our personal religious or philosophical beliefs. For example, those of us who subscribe to a traditional religious faith may be helped by thoughts such as:

I'm a child of God, created in His image, and valuable in His eyes.
My body is a temple of the Holy Spirit.
In the eyes of the Lord, I am as important as any person.
My adherence to the Golden Rule—treating others as I would have them treat me—reflects my worth as a person.

Those of us who subscribe to the philosophy of *stoicism* may benefit from functional ideas that are generated by that philosophy, such as:

What's most important is that I do my best to act honorably and do what is "right."
Although I can't change the past, I can try to accept it, forgive those who have transgressed against me, and strive for honesty and fairness.

Buddhists may be able to counter dysfunctional self-criticism by considering thoughts such as:

> My worth is best judged by my respectful treatment of all living things and my efforts to seek transcendent inner peace.

Those of us who subscribe to *deterministic philosophy* may benefit from functional thoughts that flow from that perspective, such as:

> Everything I've ever done seemed for the best at the moment. Only hindsight creates the illusion that I should or could have done better.
>
> My "weaknesses" and "failures" are entirely the result of "misfortune"—the bad luck to have been born without valued capacities, to have received insufficient nurturance and/or education, or to live in a society where my capacities are not valued.

STEPS TOWARD A REVISED SELF-IMAGE

The actions recommended here can improve our ability to recognize dysfunctional self-criticisms that have led to a negative emotional state (for example, shame, guilt, anger, fear, or despondency), as well as to respond by identifying—and focusing on—functional alternative thoughts about ourselves. These changes, in turn, can improve our emotional experience, enhance our peace of mind, inspire constructive self-assertion, and gradually achieve a more balanced and reasonable self-image.

1. Title a "page" of your *Record of Functional Thought* "Obstacles I've Overcome" and list each of the difficulties you have encountered in life, including not only traumas and losses but also family, financial, health, educational, community, societal, and personal disadvantages.

2. Title the next page of your *Record* "My Accomplishments" and list every achievement you have managed in life, no matter how humble it may seem. Include positive personal relationships formed, grades or classes completed, diplomas or certificates earned, skills attained, knowledge acquired, jobs performed, project or group involvements, anything you have built or created, property acquired, contributions of time or energy to others, etc. Works of drama often involve a protagonist who struggles to overcome many obstacles to ultimately attain success. Creating an inventory of the obstacles we have had to overcome in order to accomplish whatever we have can help us become the hero of our own story.

3. Whenever you experience shame, guilt, or anger at yourself, try to identify and record the underlying dysfunctional self-criticisms or self-doubts that prompted those feelings. Because it is best to focus as little attention as possible on dysfunctional thoughts, they should be recorded in a separate file or on the back page of your *Record*—where they won't be encountered each time you open it.

4. Generate as many functional alternative thoughts as possible, using the ideas presented in this chapter as inspiration, and record them in the location reserved for functional thoughts in your *Record*.

5. Review your *Record* with one or more trusted others (for example, close friend, sibling, mentor, therapist, religious counselor, etc.) and add any additional functional alternative thoughts, obstacles overcome, and/or accomplishments identified.

6. Keep your *Record* close at hand—somewhere you will be likely to see it each day—such as a bedside table, where you eat a meal, next to your medications, etc.—and review it at least daily, and particularly when distressed.

7. Review and revise your *Record* each time you experience shame, guilt, or anger at yourself, attempting to identify the underlying dysfunctional self-criticisms or self-doubts and generate as many functional alternative thoughts as possible—and add them to your *Record*. Then repeat steps 5 and 6.

Additional steps to take if your progress seems too slow:

1. Make an audio recording of your *Record* and listen to it once or more each day.
2. Recite your *Record* in front of a mirror once or more each day.
3. Increase the frequency with which you read your *Record* to a trusted other, making alterations and additions based on their feedback.

The more adept we become at recognizing dysfunctional self-criticisms, identifying more functional alternatives, and focusing our attention on the latter, the more our constructive actions, peace of mind, and self-image are likely to be enhanced.

4

Speaking Up

Making our desires, thoughts, and feelings known is essential for attaining our goals, earning self-respect, and enhancing our peace of mind. Without a balanced exchange of feelings and preferences, we are likely to miss opportunities, and our personal relationships can sour and fall apart. Nevertheless, the prospect of asking for what we want or expressing our opinion can bring up dysfunctional thoughts, elicit anxiety, and inhibit us from speaking up. We can become empowered, however, by learning to recognize the thoughts that inhibit our self-assertion and respond by identifying—and focusing on—functional alternatives.

CHALLENGING DYSFUNCTIONAL THOUGHTS THAT INHIBIT SELF-ASSERTION

We are sometimes prevented from expressing our feelings by a dysfunctional thought as simple as "What I think or feel isn't important enough to merit expression." When that occurs, we may be liberated by considering more reasonable and functional alternatives, such as:

People can't be expected to read my mind; others may only know what I want and how I feel if I speak up.

I'm unlikely to get what I want unless I say what I want.

It is appropriate to express my feelings and wishes, so long as I do so respectfully.

Standing up for what I want is the best (and sometimes only) way I can exert control over what happens in my life and relationships.

Keeping my feelings unspoken and hidden is likely to damage both my relationships and my self-esteem.

Self-assertion can also be inhibited by dysfunctional thoughts such as:

Saying what I want will make others think I'm selfish and demanding.

Expressing my opinion will make others think I'm arrogant and opinionated.

If I stutter or stumble over my words, I'll be humiliated and others won't take me seriously.

Expressing my feelings will just cause unnecessary conflict.

It would be awful if I offended someone by disagreeing with them or objecting to something they said or did.

Additional functional alternative thoughts that can enhance our assertiveness include:

A healthy level of "selfishness" is necessary for successful living.

I am most likely to increase my value in the eyes of myself and others by respectfully expressing my feelings and wishes.

It will be okay if I stutter or stumble over my words; almost everyone does at times and it's important that I express myself.

Expressing humility and respect for others as I assert myself will help me avoid appearing demanding, complaining, selfish, or arrogant.

Expressing my feelings will prevent them from becoming buried within and causing problems later.

If responsibly asserting my feelings upsets someone, a respectful dialogue can enable us to work through it.

It is sometimes important to make my truthful feelings and wishes
known, even if it might upset someone.

For every dysfunctional thought that inhibits us from asserting ourselves, there are reasonable and functional alternatives that offer us the
psychological freedom to take assertive action.

OUR PERFECT RIGHT

The United Nations Universal Declaration of Human Rights, drafted
by Eleanor Roosevelt, specifies that "everyone has the right to freedom
of opinion and expression" and provides us with an official list of more
functional thoughts. It specifies that our basic human rights entitle us to

1. ask for what we want (as long as we are prepared to graciously
   accept a decline).
2. say "no" to any request by another.
3. be less than perfect and make mistakes.
4. express our feelings and adopt our own values.
5. refuse responsibility for the feelings and actions of others.
6. delay a decision or change our mind.
7. walk away from, and decline to interact or associate with, any
   other person.
8. get angry, so long as we do not behave violently or abusively.

DEFINING SELF-ASSERTION

In the mental health world, assertiveness refers to the ability to express
ourselves honestly by simply stating what we want or believe *without*

disrespecting others. It means standing up for our personal rights, feelings, and beliefs in a direct and reasonable way that does not violate any other person's rights or feelings. It means confidently stating in a respectful and measured tone, "This is how I feel" or "This is what I would like."

The basic messages of assertiveness—expressed without any attempt to intimidate, humiliate, or degrade—are:

This is what I think.
This is what I'm feeling.
This is how I see the situation.
This is what I want.
This is what I prefer.

Assertiveness is the middle ground of two extremes: passivity and aggressiveness. *Passivity* involves disrespecting ourselves by failing to express honest feelings and thoughts when our interests are being disregarded *to our disadvantage.* Withholding a feeling can be a perfectly appropriate choice when we have not been harmed or disrespected. And when a conflict involves only opinion and no action that personally impacts us (for example, politics, religion, gossip about a third party, etc.), it can be best to simply change the topic of discussion with an assertive statement such as "I guess we'll have to agree to disagree on that subject" or "Can we please talk about something else?" But when our interests are negatively affected and the stakes are important to us, passivity sends counterproductive messages such as:

I don't count.
My feelings don't matter.
My thoughts aren't important.
Others can take advantage of me.

Aggression, on the other hand, involves the expression of thoughts and feelings in a way that insults or disrespects someone else. The messages of aggression are:

This is what I think and you're stupid for believing differently.
This is what I want and what you want doesn't matter.
This is what I feel and your feelings don't count.

Aggressiveness and passivity are endpoints on a continuum of response styles, with assertiveness falling in the middle. Whereas assertiveness usually involves "I" statements that communicate an internal state of the speaker ("I want . . . ," "I feel . . ."), aggressiveness typically involves "you" statements that blame ("You did . . .") or insult ("You're a . . ."). Passivity, on the other hand, usually involves making no response at all or one so weak that it is easily disregarded by others. An assertive response respects our own thoughts and feelings by sharing them, while at the same time respecting the feelings of others by avoiding blame or insult.

Passive compliance may avoid conflict, but it also may spoil an opportunity to obtain our goals. Furthermore, failing to speak up when we feel that our interests have been neglected can cause frustration, relationship damage, and diminished self-respect. Aggressiveness, on the other hand, tends to result in anger, dislike, and avoidance by others. No one likes a bully, and that's how aggressive people are viewed. Responsible assertiveness provides our best opportunity to obtain our goals while at the same time earning the respect that comes from standing up for ourself.

THE COMPONENTS OF AN ASSERTIVE STATEMENT

An assertive act can be as simple as a disapproving glance at someone who is talking during a movie or saying "excuse me" when someone is inadvertently blocking our way. Most assertive responses are simple, straightforward expressions of belief, feeling, opinion, desire, or personal rights. Examples include:

"Excuse me, I'd like to finish what I was saying."
"I'd like some time to think that over."
"I'd like my money back on this coat."
"Please lower your voice."
"Let's discuss that later in private."

Basic assertions can also involve the expression of affection or appreciation:

"I've had a good time. I'd like to see you again."
"I care for you a lot. You're very important to me.
"I'm so lucky to have a friend like you."
"You're a great teacher. I'm so glad I took your class."

Complicated situations can call for *empathic self-assertions*, responses designed to disarm and encourage compromise. These typically consist of three parts:

1. A statement of empathy that acknowledges the other person's rights or feelings.
2. A statement of the conflict and the reasons some change is wanted.
3. A statement of precisely what action we would like to occur or intend to take.

For example:

1. "I know you're under a lot of pressure . . .
2. . . . but I can't submit my proposal without your approval . . .
3. . . . so please review it within the next two days."

or

1. "I know that it's difficult to get around without a car . . .
2. . . . but I have plans for today . . .
3. . . . so I won't be able to loan you my car or drive you around."

Adding an empathic element can enhance an assertive statement by acknowledging a difficult situation or emotional bind before any conflict is addressed. This approach can be particularly useful when we are concerned that we might be viewed as selfish. The empathic statement helps us to see the other person's viewpoint while at the same time preparing the listener to be more receptive to our message, thus improving the chance for a workable compromise.

SELF-ASSERTION AND SELF-RESPECT

Even when our attempts at self-assertion do not result in the outcome we wanted, asking for what we want enhances the probability of a reasonable compromise. Perhaps even more importantly, expressing our wishes *honors* our feelings by implying that they merit consideration and diminishes feelings of helplessness. Assertiveness can challenge doubts we may have about our worth and improve our image in our own eyes and those of others.

Think of the people we most respect. Would any of them passively allow their feelings to be disrespected? Probably not. Would they speak up and call attention to their preferences? Almost certainly. Even when we do not get exactly what we want, our feelings and relationships benefit from asking that others respect our feelings, preferences, personal boundaries, and limitations. Simply knowing that we respected our own wishes enough to express them boosts our self-image. Just as we tend to respect others who stand up for themselves, standing up for ourselves increases our own self-respect.

NONVERBAL ASPECTS OF SELF-ASSERTION

There is more to being assertive than just the words we say. *How* we speak—our vocal volume and tone, facial expression, posture, gestures, eye contact, and interpersonal distance—can be vital to getting our message across. We are most likely to be perceived as assertive when our voice is appropriately loud, our eye contact is frequent but not intense, we stand upright at an appropriate distance, and we speak fluently. When our behavior is consistent with our assertive statement, the content of our message is presented more clearly.

If we are used to being accommodating, becoming more assertive may involve breaking new ground. When it is difficult to maintain eye contact, it may help to gaze instead at the forehead or chin of the person we are addressing. Or we can intermittently make brief eye contact.

Repeated rehearsal in comfortable settings can also help us deliver assertive statements smoothly and without hesitation. It may be useful to think of ourselves as actors, playing a role. By rehearsing assertive lines until we can speak them convincingly, we can begin to become more assertive. Even if we are initially just playing a role and speaking lines, the more often we respond with assertiveness, the more comfortable we are likely to become about expressing our feelings and wishes.

ESCALATING ASSERTIVENESS

When attempting to communicate assertively it is generally best to begin with the simplest, mildest, and least intrusive expression that might get our message across and then gradually elaborate if we do not get the response we hoped for. The goal is to make each successive assertion slightly firmer and more forceful, while continuing to avoid insult or threat. Escalating assertions can progress from a subtle reminder to a simple expression of preference to a firm demand to a statement of intended consequences. For example, if we are served a well-done steak after ordering it "rare," the following escalating assertion would be appropriate:

Waiter: "Is everything all right?"

Us: "I'm afraid not. I ordered my steak rare and this one is well done."

Waiter: "But I remember you saying well done."

Us: "There's apparently been a misunderstanding. Please exchange this steak for one that's rare."

Waiter: "I'm afraid there's nothing I can do about it now."

Us: "Yes there is. Please let me speak to the manager."

Forceful assertions sometimes contain a "contract option," a firm statement of the actions we intend to take should our wishes continue to be ignored. These statements convey the message that we mean business and need to be taken seriously. They differ from a threat in that they are stated in a matter-of-fact tone of voice and simply provide information about the *consequential actions* we intend to take if the conflict is not equitably resolved. Contract options often take the following form: "If you persist in . . ." or "If you refuse to . . . you'll leave me no alternative but to . . ."

Escalating assertions can also be helpful in expressing positive sentiments. For example, when the sincerity of our expression of appreciation or affection is questioned, the forcefulness of our statement can be heightened to make our feeling clearer. For example:

Us: "I want you to know how much I appreciate you and what you did for me."

Other: "Now you're being silly. It really wasn't anything."

Us: "No, I really mean it. You've been extremely helpful, and I greatly appreciate it."

KEEPING THE AIR CLEAR

Contrary to popular belief, disagreement between two assertive individuals does not usually lead to aggressive conflict. Instead, two people who are interacting assertively tend to communicate on an adult-to-adult level, openly expressing their feelings, positive and negative, while consistently displaying mutual respect. The result of such an interaction is typically either

1. a workable compromise, in which each party agrees to sacrifice something so that the wishes of both can be respected, or
2. a respectable impasse, where no compromise is reached but each person understands the other's position and his or her right to hold it.

A mutually assertive interaction usually results in a feeling of having engaged in meaningful dialogue with someone worthy of our trust and respect who also considers us worthy of such. It is often useful to openly express our respect and concern for the relationship (for example, "You know that I think of you like family and I wouldn't want anything to change that").

SOME CAUTIONS ABOUT ASSERTIVENESS

1. Although typically for the best, self-assertion is never guaranteed to get what we want. We will frequently find it necessary to be graceful in response to an assertive refusal. Although it is our right to express our wishes, others also have a right to decline and to expect that their wishes will also be considered. Our reward for being assertive may be simply knowing that we honored our feelings by making them known.
2. Not all truthful statements represent responsible assertion. Expressions that are likely to be perceived as insulting or that un-

necessarily call attention to a person's weakness or sensitivity are aggressive, not assertive. When used as a "blunt weapon," even an honest and truthful statement can be aggressive, insulting, or embarrassing under the pretext of good faith assertion.

3. Statements beginning "I think . . . ," "I feel . . . ," "I believe . . . ," or even "I wish . . ." can be aggressive rather than assertive when they express criticism or insult (for example, "I think you're an idiot" or "I wish you were as pretty as your sister").

4. Assertiveness is appropriate only when dealing with a reasonable person. As soon as the person with whom we are interacting acts unreasonably (for example, displays aggressiveness, lewdness, or irrationality), our only reasonable course of action is to politely end the interaction and remove ourselves from the situation. There are limits beyond which continuing to be assertive is inappropriate.

5. Disagreeing with another person's *opinion* is a special case of assertiveness and calls for careful treading. It is for good reason that politics and religion are usually considered subjects to avoid in general conversation. Strongly held opinions or beliefs are rarely changed by even the most well-reasoned arguments, and presenting them can quickly lead to conflict and impasse. This is because we tend to meet challenges to our views by finding reasons to strengthen, rather than weaken, them. Tactfulness often dictates that we avoid sensitive matters or try to change the subject when they arise.

6. It is important to remember that there is a huge difference between anger and aggression. Anger is a normal emotion. Aggression occurs when anger is expressed abusively. The impulsive expression of anger, without sufficient consideration of how it may impact others, represents aggression.

7. Aggression sometimes occurs because we fail to express a complaint and passively ignore our anger until it has become overwhelming. It is best to express anger before it grows to unmanageable proportions and when we are able to fully engage our rational thought processes.

8. When we have tended to be overly passive, attempts to become more assertive may result in pressure from others to resume our usual more compliant behavior. In such cases, a technique called the "broken record" can help us persist at being assertive. This involves selecting one or two thoughts that express our position and stating only those ideas in response to whatever is said. For example, when a friend inconveniently announces that he is coming by to drop off his dog because he has suddenly been called out of town, we might respond, "I'm sorry, but I won't be able to help you out this time. . . . I hope you find someone who can." If our refusal is not readily accepted, we simply repeat the same or a similar assertion ("I can tell that you're in a pinch and I'm sorry that I can't accommodate you like I did before"), refusing to be manipulated into accepting an unwanted responsibility.

9. We sometimes feel pressured to respond immediately to a request for assistance, and if we are in the habit of pleasing others it can be easiest to acquiesce. In such circumstances it is acceptably assertive to ask for additional time to further consider the matter. Statements such as "Give me a few minutes to think about that" or "I'd like to sleep on that" are reasonable self-assertions that are relatively simple and unthreatening. They can also relieve the immediate pressure that might otherwise lead us to acquiesce out of habit and give us an opportunity to create and rehearse a response based on reflection and reason.

EXAMPLES OF RESPONSIBLE ASSERTIVE STATEMENTS

To a salesperson or solicitor at the door or on the phone:

I'm sorry, but I don't buy anything [give anything to] from someone who comes to my door.
I'm not interested. Please remove my name and number from your list.

I need more information. I'd like to speak to a supervisor (or "I need some time to research the issue").

To a friend or loved one who asks an inconvenient favor:

I'm so sorry, I won't be able to help you out this time. I hope you find someone who can.

Let me check my schedule and think about that. I'll get back to you in a few minutes. (Followed later by "I'm so sorry, I won't be able to help you out this time. I hope you find someone who can.")

This afternoon doesn't work for me. Is there some other time that would work?

I'm sorry to have to disappoint you, but I won't be able to. . . . Can you think of someone else who might be able to?

To someone we may have upset:

I can see that I've upset you. Please tell me what you're feeling so we can try to work this out.

Please lower your voice. I'm sorry I upset you but yelling at me will only make things worse.

Can we please discuss this later in private?

I value our relationship very much and want to earn your trust again.

I didn't mean to upset you. I'll try to be more considerate of your feelings in the future.

I'm sorry that I inconvenienced you, but my appointment today took much longer than anticipated. Please let me make it up to you by . . .

To someone who has upset us:

I hear what you're saying, but I'm most comfortable doing it my way. So please respect the decision I've made.

Before I say something I don't mean, I'm going to leave for a while and cool down.

I don't like the way this conversation is going. Can we please talk about something else?

What you said makes me feel like you don't care about my feelings; that hurts because I want you to care as much about mine as I care about yours.

Please believe that I'm telling you the truth. When you respond skeptically, it feels like you're calling me a liar.

Please ask before committing me to something.

I was expecting you much earlier. What happened?

I know that you want the best for me, but your advice sometimes feels like criticism. Please be more careful when you feel like weighing in.

Please don't criticize me in front of others. If you have an issue with something I've done, please bring it up when we're by ourselves.

Please just leave me alone right now. I need some time to myself.

Please ask for my input before making decisions that affect both of us.

To someone you want to support:

I'm sure you'll find a good way to deal with that problem. Let me know if I can help.

I want you to know I believe in you and will support whatever decision you make.

To a doctor, attorney, or other professional advisor:

Many of my phone calls haven't been returned and I need to feel more connected. Please provide me with an email address or text number where you would be sure to get my messages.

I've decided I want this issue taken care of as soon as possible. Please contact me or make an appointment for me to see you, whichever would be necessary.

I'm confused about my legal case/medical condition. Please let me know your opinion, what I can expect, and what you recommend.

I understand that you're very busy, but it's crucial to me that you get my medications/surgery/repairs authorized as soon as possible.

Unless you show me that my case is important to you, I'll have no choice but to find another attorney/doctor.

To someone we appreciate:

I want you to know that I really appreciate what you've done for me. You deserve a lot of credit.

I want you to know that I'm fully committed to this relationship. I'll do all I can to make it work and I hope you'll do the same.

FINDING THE BEST MESSAGE

It can be challenging to find a self-assertion that is likely to be effective in difficult situations. When our message is likely to be unwelcome, the words we choose and our presentation become even more important. We are likely to be most effective if we take the following steps *before* we speak:

1. *Get the facts.* Find out as much as possible about the situation: who, what, where, when, why, and how.
2. *Identify objectives.* Is the intention to simply impart bad news or to end a relationship? Or is there also a wish to provide comfort and direction?
3. *Address your own emotions.* How does it feel to be taking this action? What might be done to ease the distress?

4. *Practice aloud.* Rehearse the desired words and tone. Record and listen to the communication, looking for ways it might be improved.

STEPS TOWARD BECOMING MORE ASSERTIVE

1. Head a page or file in your *Record of Functional Thought* "Responsible Assertiveness."
2. Each time you find yourself upset about having made an excessively passive or aggressive response—or not having responded at all and wishing you had—record as many functional thoughts as you can that explain why assertiveness was appropriate, using this chapter as reference and inspiration.
3. Record as many responsibly assertive responses to the situation as you can identify, again using this chapter as reference and inspiration.
4. Review the functional thoughts and assertive statements you have recorded in your *Record* with one or more trusted others and alter or add functional thoughts and assertive statements based on the feedback you receive.
5. Practice making the assertive responses you have recorded, speaking to yourself in a mirror.
6. Record a video of yourself making the assertive statements, review the recording, and make changes that would make the statements more compelling.
7. Role-play each scenario in which you wished you had been more assertive with a trusted other and ask for that person's feedback about how you might come across more effectively.

5

Making the Most of Relationships

Attachments to others often create our most powerful emotions. We are social animals, programmed to bond. Most of us rate our personal relationships as primary in importance—ahead of careers, accomplishments, fame, or wealth. A loving relationship can make us feel more "connected," "grounded," and "centered" than any other experience. Even absent a sexual element, physical contact with those we care about is usually critical to our well-being. Support from a network of friends and relatives can get us through our worst moments. Joy can be found in being goofy with other goofballs who enjoy, or at least tolerate, our goofiness. In later life, our most common wish is that we had spent more time with the people we care for most.

Although they can be complicated and difficult—and can cause intense emotional pain when they go wrong—personal relationships often provide the best opportunity to enhance the quality of our lives. No matter how discouraged we may feel about making positive connections, we can establish successful relationships if we make them a priority, reasonably negotiate compromises to resolve conflicts, and consistently display the respect and understanding that we would want for ourselves.

THE INGREDIENTS OF
A FUNCTIONAL RELATIONSHIP

Five elements are usually required for any type of relationship to survive and thrive:

1. General agreement on what the relationship is to be—its nature, form, and scope.
2. A commitment of time and energy sufficient to meet each other's expectations.
3. Mutual respect communicated by giving as much consideration to the other's preferences, wishes, and feelings as we expect for our own.
4. Responsible assertive communication of honest feelings and wishes—without aggression, threats, insults, or other forms of disrespectful behavior.
5. Tolerance and acceptance of each other's innocent idiosyncrasies, normal human faults and weaknesses, and sincerely regretted mistakes.
6. Respect for each other's interpersonal boundaries (for example, personal space, personal business, individual responsibilities, etc.).
7. A bilateral commitment to negotiate in good faith to find compromises that can resolve the conflicts that inevitably arise.

Compromise—the ability to negotiate and reach agreements seen as fair by each person—is often the key to successful relationships. Conflicts arise frequently, and when an acceptable resolution cannot be negotiated, it may be in the best interest of the relationship to seek resolution using a decision-making system that both participants consider fair, such as the flip of a coin. We can often accept an outcome we dislike if we know that our interests were given equal weight in reaching it. If either participant continues to be unhappy with the result, a different solution can be proposed, but with the understanding that the fairly reached "compromise" will stand unless both participants agree on another.

THE SOCIAL SUPPORT NETWORK

Although most of us hope to find a spouse or life partner, establishing a healthy *social support network*—the group of friends and relatives with whom we have formed meaningful connections—can be equally important. These relationships can enrich our lives and help us cope with whatever trouble may come our way. The extent and quality of our social support network has been found to accurately predict how well we adjust to major loss or trauma. Furthermore, successful experiences in friendship and/or familial relationships can better prepare us for the challenges of a more comprehensive relationship, as well as possibly relieving the pressure a primary partner might feel when expected to meet all our interpersonal needs.

Some of us choose to live without a primary loving relationship, instead finding satisfaction and meaning in career pursuits, avocational interests, and/or other relationships. Even those of us who want a primary loving relationship will usually benefit from first establishing a full and rewarding independent life, including

1. a social support network of friends and/or family members, people that we see or communicate with on a regular basis, with whom we share mutual regard, and who provide support in times of crisis or loss;
2. a set of interests and activities that keep us active and self-expressive (for example, cooking, painting, crafts, dance, writing, politics, faith-based activities, competitive games, etc.);
3. positive self-care habits—such as exercise, diet, and participating in our own medical care when indicated; and
4. becoming self-supporting.

We become much more attractive as a potential loving relationship partner *after* we have developed a fulfilling life as a single person, with a social support network, occupation or career attainment or potential, and/or a variety of avocational interests and activities. Ironically, primary loving relationships are more likely to succeed when we *need* them less than we *want* them.

LOVING RELATIONSHIPS

In Western culture, the word *love* is used for several different feelings. The loving relationships presented in music and drama are usually of the "fell in love" variety, a temporary biology-induced state of hormonal excitement and infatuation. A "mature loving relationship," on the other hand, is a long-term mutual commitment by two adults to put each other's interests and feelings above those of any other person and only *slightly beneath* their own.

The "falling in love" state is passive and temporary; it happens to us and—unless it changes into a more mature loving relationship—it will eventually end. In contrast, a "loving relationship" is consciously created by two people and lasts as long they decide to keep it alive. Whereas a loving relationship facilitates constructive efforts and helps us grow to our full potential, having "fallen in love" often causes us to become distracted and preoccupied with ourselves and can impair our ability to function. Whereas a loving relationship causes us to feel grateful and generous, immature romantic "love" can cause us to be selfish and jealous. Although falling in love can be a powerful intoxicant, it is far more likely to enrich our lives and enhance our peace of mind after it evolves into a mature loving relationship.

Though we tend to think of a primary loving relationship as one involving two sexually exclusive partners who live together, the details and boundaries depend on the compromises we negotiate. Sexual intimacy, although usual, is not an essential element of every loving relationship.

Relationships often begin when two people experience the automatic biological reaction of "falling in love." Physical attraction can set off hormonal "fireworks" that produce an intoxication rivaling that of any drug. If the person to whom we are attracted reciprocates, the relationship is underway. If we prove to have *compatible attitudes and values*, the infatuation can last for months as we "discover" each other. The relationship is likely to develop into a mature loving relationship, however, only if the participants also happen to *meet each other's needs* (for example, for giving and receiving affection, assuming and relinquishing control, interacting with and withdrawing from others, acquiring and managing resources, having children, etc.).

Although being loved or accommodated by another person can be extremely pleasurable, the greatest reward of a loving relationship comes from being part of something greater than ourselves. Union with another can enhance the joy and humor of life while at the same time easing its inevitable pain and sorrow.

A mature loving relationship is formed when we make a mutual commitment to be partners, support each other as equals, respect each other's feelings and desires, and tolerate each other's many faults and weaknesses. The content and boundaries of our relationships are defined by the compromises we negotiate. Relationships fail when compromise cannot be attained.

Primary loving relationships require all the ingredients necessary for any relationship to thrive *plus* a commitment by each partner to treat the relationship as a precious possession and confront the world as "a team of two." This means

1. consulting our partner before making any decision that may affect "the team,"
2. supporting each other's efforts to meet personal goals and optimally thrive, and
3. not permitting anyone to come between or "split" the partners by playing one against the other. It is particularly important that parents deal with their children as a team, making and presenting decisions about rules, limits, and consequences as a team. Children can sense—and will attempt to take advantage of—any division between parents by setting one against the other.

RELATIONSHIP MAINTENANCE

Conflicts arise in every relationship and resolving them requires that each partner contribute the time and energy to share feelings, actively listen, and negotiate compromises in a respectful manner. Potential solutions exist for almost every relationship problem but can sometimes be discovered only when the participants tenderly consider each other's feelings and reasonably balance them against their own.

As Tolstoy points out in the opening lines of *Anna Karenina*, healthy family relations are rare because they require successful management of each of the many potential sources of family strife. Chances are that something will go wrong in at least a few realms of family life, meaning that it is normal for us to encounter discord with even those we love most.

The first rule of attaining a positive relationship with family members is to *limit the opportunity for discord*. The less contact we have with people who are often obnoxious the better, whether relatives or not. When required to be at the same event, we can keep our distance and avoid doing or saying anything that might trigger an unwanted response. We can be consistently cordial and polite, and if someone speaks or acts offensively we can attempt to redirect the conversation toward a more neutral topic. If obnoxious behavior persists, we can excuse ourselves and leave.

Problems often arise when we try to "prove" to someone that our belief or point of view is better or more accurate than theirs. The result frequently is that we prove only that we value our need to be right more than we value the relationship and the other person's feelings. It is possible for competitive individuals to have successful relationships, but only when they can put the goals of the "team" ahead of personal goals. For the relationship to "win," both partners must feel that their interests have been respected. When one partner feels cheated or disrespected by the outcome of a conflict, the relationship loses.

When no acceptable compromise can be negotiated, it can be best to settle differences by random chance, such as the flip of a coin. The relationship is most likely to thrive when each partner feels that their wishes have been given equal weight in making decisions and that the relationship itself is the priority.

Before opening a dialogue likely to involve conflict, we may benefit by considering the following questions:

1. Could my anger be about something else that I am more upset about than this particular issue?
2. Is this my business? Am I acting on behalf of someone else who might be best allowed to address the issue?
3. Is expressing this grievance *worth* the risk of creating conflict or provoking anger?
4. How might I introduce this concern to minimize the conflict?

RULES OF FAIR FIGHTING

Discussions about sensitive relationship issues can sometimes devolve into bitter arguments that accomplish little but injured feelings. A dialogue is more likely to be productive if commonly accepted "ground rules" such as those listed here can be agreed upon in advance. When a rule is violated, the violation should be pointed out and the rule should be reviewed before the dialogue is resumed.

1. *Both partners must be willing to talk.* Provided our partner's behavior remains respectful, "stonewalling"—refusing to participate— usually represents a passive-aggressive attempt to frustrate and annoy. It is best prohibited.
2. *Each partner has the right to withdraw.* If feeling threatened or in danger of losing self-control, either participant can interrupt the discussion, disengage from the conflict, and leave the premises.
3. *One issue is to be discussed at a time.* Once a complaint has been raised, discussion of any other issue or event—especially those that occurred more than twenty-four hours earlier—should be avoided until both partners agree to take up a new topic of discussion.

4. *Others should be left out of the dialogue.* With the exception of a neutral relationship counselor or therapist, dragging others into a relationship dialogue is best prohibited, either as a participant or a subject of discussion. The dialogue should focus on the actions of the two partners.

5. *Violence is never to be tolerated.* Any violent act, including self-harm or property damage, must be considered unacceptable. The discussion should be immediately ended, each partner should seek refuge and safety, and appropriate authorities should be notified.

6. *Comments should be assertive, not aggressive.* Insults, threats, and yelling are prohibited. Instead of blaming or making accusations, the problem and the desired change should be stated (for example, "I feel like I never catch up with household tasks, and I'd like you to assume more responsibility").

7. *Generalizations should be avoided.* Statements beginning "You always . . ." or "You never . . ." or negative comparisons such as "You're just like . . ." provoke defensiveness and are almost always less than completely accurate.

8. *Behavior should be addressed rather than character.* "It upset me when you took my car without asking" rather than "I hate your selfishness." "Please stop yelling" is likely to work better than "I wish you weren't such a bully."

9. *Compromise is better than "winning."* The primary goals should be reaching a compromise and enhancing the relationship. Remember that when one participant "wins," the other is left wounded and the relationship suffers.

10. *Remember that listening is even more important than speaking.* Each partner should have a turn to talk without being interrupted. A time limit for speaking may help. Before presenting your point of view, make sure your partner has finished speaking and that you understood what they said, no matter how much you might disagree. "Feeling heard" soothes injured feelings more than any argument can.

FINDING THE RIGHT WORDS

Within valued relationships, it is especially important to avoid statements that might be construed as aggressive, while at the same time looking for opportunities to express appreciation and confidence. Although criticism is sometimes called "constructive," rarely are critical remarks appreciated, and they frequently result in conflict. We can sometimes avoid putting a friend or partner on the defensive by asking for what we want (for example, "When you leave the house, please let me know where you're going and when I can expect you back") rather than making a complaint or criticism. Even when criticism may be justified, it is often best left unexpressed unless it can be phrased in the form of a request for specific actions by our partner.

Expressing positive regard is difficult for many of us but often enhances a relationship, especially when reciprocated. Most of us cherish compliments and expressions of affection (for example, "You're a great mom," "Your carbonara is the best," "I love you," "I'm so lucky to have you in my life," etc.), confidence (for example, "You'll be great," "I'm certain that you'll figure out the best thing to do," etc.), or solidarity (for example, "We've become a team of two and whatever is good for you is therefore also good for me," "I want you to go watch football with your friends because I know it's important to you and that makes it important to me," etc.).

When a loved one's behavior disappoints us, providing an example of the language or actions we would have preferred can be a relatively inoffensive and potentially effective response. For example, when we are wanting expressions of affection, appreciation, understanding, or confidence, we might offer an example of the words we would like to hear (for example, "When I seem to be distressed please say something like 'I'm sorry that you're upset, but you know that I'm 100 percent behind you, I'm sure you'll overcome this problem, and I'll always be here for you'"). Providing direction and rewarding behavior we prefer is likely to achieve better results than would criticism alone.

The well-being of a relationship sometimes depends on our ability to considerately express wishes, dissatisfactions, and injured feelings. When conflict arises, the relationship is most likely to benefit from both partners "putting their cards on the table," negotiating reasonably, and forging compromise—while consistently displaying respect for each other's feelings and the relationship itself. Relationships work best when we primarily represent our own interests but also strive to make sure that our partner also feels that their feelings have been taken into consideration. If both partners are willing to reasonably negotiate and compromise, some workable resolution is likely to be found—even if it may be only to respectfully agree to disagree.

Self-assertion is especially important in the context of a loving relationship because unaddressed frustrations can do significant damage. Although it is sometimes tempting to overlook unreasonable behavior to avoid conflict, passive tolerance usually does more damage than would respectfully calling attention to it. Quietly overlooking unacceptable actions can unintentionally signal permission to ignore our feelings. Unexpressed anger that is "swallowed," furthermore, often resurfaces as anxiety or a psychosomatic ailment (for example, headache or gastritis) or causes us to act in ways that irritate our partner without being directly hostile.

Passive-aggressive behaviors (for example, keeping others waiting, seeming to be distracted during a serious discussion, smiling when being presented with a complaint, etc.) are expressions of frustration that usually cause irritation but often go unnoticed (or, if noticed, are easy to justify). To resolve relationship problems and diminish conflict in general, it is best to respectfully call attention to irritating behavior while consistently communicating the message "I want to bring this matter to your attention so that we can get it resolved because you and our relationship are important to me."

I'M OKAY, YOU'RE OKAY

Outside of organizations with structured hierarchies (for example, military, police, businesses, schools, religious organizations, etc.), our communications are most likely to be effective when we address others as equal adults and expect similar treatment in return. This means being sincere, respectful, understanding, forthright, and assertive. Neither threats, blame, insults, cursing, commands, scolding, nor begging constitute adult-to-adult communication as each implies a hierarchy inconsistent with a positive personal relationship.

When we speak "down" to another adult over whom we have no special authority (as might a parent or teacher to a child), we are likely to elicit child-like responses, either rebellious or dependent. When another person inappropriately speaks down to us, our best hope of evoking more appropriate behavior is to attempt a sincere adult-to-adult assertive response. Thus, when someone we value offensively tells us how we "should" respond to a stressful circumstance, we might be able to provoke a more mature conversation by responding, "I'll take your advice into consideration in making my decision." If the other person continues to speak from a position of superiority, it would probably be best to either completely disengage or inquire about their inappropriate stance of authority.

TOLERANCE AND FORGIVING

Despite our best efforts, each of us sometimes disturb or offend others. For this reason, developing and maintaining good personal relationships sometimes depends on our abilities to apologize, forgive, overlook, tolerate, and learn to laugh about our actions and those of our relationship partners. A relationship can survive many minor transgressions when both partners want it to survive and are willing to work at doing better.

Being severely disappointed by someone we care about can evoke intense emotional pain and sometimes highlights our worst characteristics. The prospect of losing a relationship partner or one's place in a family can be so overwhelming that it can cause some of us to become irrational—and a few to become dangerous. *Any display or threat of violence (including self-harm and destruction of property) must be taken seriously*. Anyone who might be in harm's way should immediately seek a safe environment and law enforcement authorities should be notified (911 in the United States). Most communities have shelters or safe houses that can be located through the National Domestic Violence Hotline (800-799-7233 or 800-799-SAFE or thehotline.org), which provides twenty-four-hour advice and assistance. Although it is natural that we are reluctant to involve "outsiders" in a personal dispute, failure to take decisive action in the face of violence is often taken as a signal that dangerous behavior will be tolerated, making it more likely that violence will recur.

When a relationship partner appears to be unable to stop a pattern of destructive behavior and is unwilling to participate in an appropriate management program, the most constructive step for both partners is to end the relationship. Healthy detachment is the art of lovingly letting go of what we cannot control. *Sometimes the best way we can express our love is to allow the one we love to encounter the natural consequences of their behavior.* Completely withdrawing from a relationship is sometimes the only way we can refuse to condone or "enable" a loved one's self-destructive behavior. There are also twelve-step programs (for example, Al-Anon, Codependents Anonymous, etc.) for those of us who are struggling to cope with a loved one's self-destructive behavior.

When we have upset a relationship partner, we often make the mistake of attempting to defend ourselves (for example, "You're just too sensitive," "I didn't do anything wrong," "What about the time you . . . ?"). Although this impulse is natural, it is rarely helpful and often escalates the conflict. Our relationships will usually benefit most when we express remorse that we caused our partner distress and display motivation to prevent a recurrence. It rarely serves us to suggest that someone should not be feeling as they do. A potentially helpful response would be something like "I'm sorry if I offended you; I didn't mean to cause you distress; I'll do my best to avoid upsetting you like that again."

STAYING IN OUR LANE

Relationship conflict can result when one participant fails to respect the other's personal boundaries. We tend to interact best when we avoid intrusions into each other's personal business, problems, and outside relationships. The more frequently we cross personal boundaries, the greater the potential for conflict.

Although it is natural to want to help or protect those we care about, when we deal with other adults it is usually best to avoid speaking for them, directing their actions, or attempting to rescue them from problems created by their own decisions and actions. Assuming responsibility for another person's business can be tempting because it places us in the role of *rescuer* and distracts us from our own problems and the anxiety they may arouse. The relationship, however, is likely to suffer. We will often find it impossible to solve someone else's problem and may neglect our own affairs in making the effort. Furthermore, if the other person accepts our intrusion into what should be their business, they are likely to be either angered by the implication that they lack the competence to handle their own affairs or increasingly dependent on us. Although we may initially see the other person as a "victim" and ourselves as their "rescuer," when they become irritated or unreasonably dependent, we are likely to begin feeling like the "victim" and viewing them as the "villain." And when we become unable or unwilling to provide further rescue, our relationship partner is likely to see us as a "villain." These rapidly shifting roles of the "victim-rescuer-villain triangle" are a frequent result of crossing boundaries and frequently what causes us to seek therapy.

Even if we might occasionally appreciate assistance from friends or family, most of us do not want to be "helped" with tasks that we can handle on our own. Accepting help can suggest that we are somehow incompetent or that our "helper" is somehow superior. Thus, we may resent anyone we come to rely on for "help." Adults who become dependent on monetary allotments from wealthy parents tend to develop mixed feelings about their parents. They appreciate the concern but resent being dependent. Adult relationships function best when the participants each feel competent and independent.

It is impossible to "fix" another person and it is a mistake to enter a relationship with the expectation that that we can. People change, but the nature and timing of that change is unpredictable and almost never under our control. Unless we observe compelling evidence that change is taking place, the wisest course is to make decisions based on the assumption that another person will *not* change. If we later observe positive changes, we can reconsider our options.

Most professional organizations have a provision in their ethical standards specifying that "confounded relationships" are to be avoided. A relationship becomes "confounded" when we adopt a second relationship with someone with whom we already have a relationship. Each new connection increases the probability that conflict in one relationship will contaminate the other relationship. Every new relationship aspect (for example, a business partnership with our father-in-law, a golf partnership with our doctor, hiring a neighbor to provide personal services, etc.) makes it more difficult to maintain the health of that relationship. This phenomenon explains why siblings often become estranged when they also become competitors for their parents' estate and why relationships with people we see often (for example, coworkers, classmates, neighbors, a good friend's sister, etc.) can become very awkward if the relationship does not work out—or even if it does. Relationships function best when kept as "clean" and narrowly defined as possible.

One of the reasons we tend to have most conflict with our primary loving partners is that those relationships are inherently confounded, with connections as friends, lovers, housemates, companions, financial partners, coparents, etc. Each of these relationship aspects magnifies the opportunity for conflict. Although being in a loving relationship can create the wonderful feeling that we have become part of something beyond ourselves, when two lives begin overlapping, the boundaries that separate our loved one's concerns from our own can become blurred. This is especially true for those of us who have grown up in a home where there was little respect for personal boundaries and family members frequently intruded into each other's affairs. This type of childhood experience can result in an unfortunate adult tendency to inject ourselves into our partner's personal business in a manner that can be perceived as intrusive.

Getting our needs met and resolving our own issues is our personal responsibility. Loving relationships work best when each of us pursues happiness in our own way while at the same time consistently displaying respect for our partner's feelings and the boundaries between our personal business. This often means deciding what we want to do and who we want to see and then taking our partner's plans and wishes into consideration as we proceed. It also means understanding that anything that is good for our partner is probably also good for the relationship if we can be generous about endorsing—or at least tolerating—it. Few things enhance affection as much as observing that our partner values our happiness even when it may be inconvenient for them.

SHAPING BEHAVIOR

Although we cannot change another person, we can sometimes influence their actions. In the context of a loving relationship direct requests for what we want are often effective, especially when made assertively and sincerely. We may also be able to elicit behavior more to our liking by being careful to make sure that actions that approximate what we want are rewarded (or "reinforced") and that actions that less resemble what we hope for are not rewarded. Although this may sound like manipulation, behavioral psychologists call it "shaping," and it is employed in most educational programs. Whether we try to influence outcomes or not, our behavior is constantly being altered by its results.

Our actions are based on the outcomes of our previous actions. We do what we expect will be most likely to produce a result we desire. This means that we can be encouraged—and can encourage others—to take a desired action if we can alter expectations about the outcome.

The behavior we hope for is more likely to occur if we can *increase* the expectation that it will be rewarded. Conversely, we may be able to diminish the likelihood of unwanted behavior if we can *decrease* the expectation of positive results.

This simple behavioral law has long been known and used in daily life, though sometimes without recognition. For example, we express our gratitude and repay favors in the hope of eliciting more desired responses. By becoming more mindful of the impact our actions can have on our significant others, we may be able to avoid inadvertently discouraging behavior we want, encouraging behavior we do not want, or sending an inconsistent message. For example, giving a great deal of attention—or ice cream—to a child who is throwing a tantrum can inadvertently encourage more tantrums. And telling someone that their behavior is unacceptable and will not be tolerated without taking any consistent action (for example, separating, consulting a therapist, etc.) can instead send the message that such behavior will be tolerated. We are most effective when our words and behavior reinforce each other.

WHEN TO END A RELATIONSHIP

Most relationships that have been successful at some point in time have not been impacted by violence can be rehabilitated. Although the "grass often looks greener" elsewhere and the initial stages of a new relationship can be exciting, a relationship with a different partner may be no more likely to succeed, especially if our behavior has played a role in precipitating conflict.

Some transgressions are common and minor enough that they can usually be survived if both partners are willing to work toward improving the relationship. Frequent sources of relationship conflict that can often be resolved by sincere discussion or couples counseling include

1. unreasonable or unnecessary arguing,
2. excessive criticism,

3. paying inappropriate attention to a third person,
4. "dumping" negative emotions onto our partner because they are available and "safe,"
5. expecting more than is fair from our partner, and
6. making decisions that impact our partner without consulting them.

Relationships constantly change and primary loving relationships often spiral, sometimes for the better and sometimes for the worse. By the time a couple enters counseling, their relationship has often spiraled downward to the point that they are caught up in a "toxic loop" of hostile communication. It may seem as though the two partners are on opposite sides of a battle line launching verbal assaults back and forth.

The first goal in attempting to repair a damaged relationship is to establish a "ceasefire," a mutual agreement to refrain from further attacks. Only when two people can address each other respectfully is it possible to address conflicts effectively, halt hostile exchanges, and initiate a pattern of positive communication. Research has shown that two people judge their relationship "successful" when their dialogue contains at least five times as many positive as negative expressions. An important step in repairing a damaged relationship, therefore, is replacing hostile communications with expressions of consideration, respect, and caring.

As indicated by the approximately 50 percent divorce rate in the United States, however, many attempts to repair a loving relationship fail. No matter how hard we might try to make a relationship work, it is likely to fail unless the other person is also committed. The option of ending a relationship is essential because it can prevent us from becoming "trapped" in an unhealthy situation. Troublesome aspects of another's personality may not be evident at the beginning of the relationship. We sometimes become so excited and hopeful about a relationship that we are "blind" to signs that the other person may not be an appropriate relationship partner. We also sometimes enter relationships with the unrealistic notion that we will be able to change the other person.

Relationships that have been affected by substance abuse, domestic violence, or other recurrent aggressive or self-defeating actions are difficult—and sometimes impossible—to salvage. Tolerance, acceptance, and forgiveness can only go so far. Neither physical abuse nor repeated verbal abuse or humiliation should be tolerated. And no one should be required to assume all the bulk of household responsibilities because their partner is engaging in a pattern of self-destructive behavior.

Although serious relationship offenses (for example, sexual cheating, violence, criminal behavior, etc.) can be "deal breakers" that place the survival of the relationship in doubt, loving relationships can survive many storms provided

1. *both* individuals are willing to work to make the relationship survive,
2. remorse is sincerely displayed,
3. amends are made, and
4. forgiveness is valued and available.

When the offense has been major, survival of the relationship is also likely to depend on great patience—by the offended partner to observe the offender's remorse and amends and by the offending partner to tolerate the offended partner's reactive hostility and distrust.

Substance abuse is one of the most common reasons that relationships fail. No one who is abusing drugs or alcohol is capable of reasonably participating in a relationship or benefiting from any effort to improve a relationship, including counseling or psychotherapy. A relationship that is faltering because of destructive behavior (for example, substance abuse, domestic violence, compulsive gambling, infidelity, criminal activity, etc.) can be salvaged only if *both* partners acknowledge that the behavior is unacceptable, it is immediately and completely discontinued, and the transgressor seeks appropriate help (for example, detox and rehab, medical treatment, anger management, Alcoholics Anonymous or some other twelve-step program, etc.). If those conditions are not met, remaining in a relationship with someone who has displayed a pattern of self-destructive behavior is likely to result in further damage to both the relationship and each participant.

When we realize that a relationship is unlikely to ever function as we had hoped, the option of getting out and pursuing a rewarding single life or establishing a better relationship can be crucial to our well-being. No matter how upsetting relationship problems might become, it is usually best to avoid mentioning "separation" or "divorce" until a final decision has been made. Unless we have a plan and intend to move out or ask our partner to move out, it is best to focus our energy on resolving the conflicts. Mentioning separation or divorce to a partner before a decision has actually been made is likely to escalate the conflict and evoke so much negative emotion that it may become impossible to constructively work together.

When a partner's actions have raised suspicions of betrayal that might end the relationship, it may be important that we research our legal and financial rights and responsibilities *before* making any accusation. It may even make sense to meet with an attorney who specializes in family law. Becoming informed does not mean that we are abandoning hope of saving the partnership, only that we want to understand our options and be prepared for all possibilities.

Once the decision has been made to end a relationship, it is important to avoid sending "mixed signals." Both participants are likely to benefit from a consistent message that the relationship is over and the future life of each will not involve the other. Because we are likely to be emotionally vulnerable when ending a relationship and may still have considerable concern for our partner's well-being, we may be tempted to provide or seek comfort. Doing either, however, is likely to create confusion, increase the overall amount of emotional pain, and heighten angry feelings. When the partner ending a relationship is ambivalent and sends mixed messages (for example, continuing to communicate after asking for no further contact, delaying a move out, continuing to discuss relationship issues, etc.), frustration can become magnified. Although it may be possible for former relationship partners to become "friends," that usually can occur *only after* each has adjusted to the separation and developed a stable life as a single or in a new relationship.

When it is our partner who ends the relationship, the best we can do is try to respect the decision, accept that a long-term relationship was not meant to be, and try to be thankful that we can avoid wasting any more time and energy on a lost cause and can begin making the most of an independent life. This often means turning to our social support network (friends, family members, clergy, a therapist, etc.) to keep us involved and active and help us work through the grief and anger usually associated with rejection. Refusing to accept a partner's decision to end a relationship is like repeatedly expressing jealousy during a relationship—it achieves nothing worthwhile and makes us seem disrespectful, pathetic, or disturbed.

STEPS TOWARD BETTER RELATIONSHIPS

If you want to expand your social support network:

1. On a new page or file of your *Record of Functional Thought*, make a list of "Relatives, Friends, Associates, and Acquaintances." Then rate from one to five each person's potential to become a more significant part of your social support network. Take into consideration availability, positive and negative personal qualities, and how much you would like to spend more time with them. Then reach out to those with the highest ratings to suggest a casual meeting: coffee, lunch, a hike, a drink, attending an event. Be guided by their responses. If your invitation is accepted, be prepared to discuss noncontroversial topics such as sports, TV shows, and positive reminiscences. If that goes well, explore the other person's interest in further interactions. When uncertain about how to proceed, consider seeking the input of a close friend, family member, therapist, or personal advisor.

2. On a new page or file of your *Record* begin a list of "Opportunities for Involvement" and add to it any and all possibilities you identify. Search for groups of people likely to share your interests and attitudes. Consider book clubs (almost every library branch sponsors one), religious organizations, volunteer opportunities, and especially associations related to your interests, whether in cars, birds, pets, hiking, cycling, politics, or something else. The website meetup.com provides information about almost every public organization and meeting in every community with details about how to get involved. At such meetings look for commonalities between yourself and other attendees with the goal of developing friendships.

If you are looking for a primary loving relationship:

1. First become the best relationship candidate possible by establishing healthy independence.
   a. Build a healthy social support network using the steps described earlier.
   b. Work toward resolving your unwanted habits and improving your circumstances; we all have issues to work on.
   c. Enhance your potential for a primary partnership by taking care of yourself and becoming as financially independent and secure as possible.
   d. If you have recently had a relationship fail, try to figure out what went wrong and how you might alter behaviors that may have contributed to that failure.
2. Get involved and let others know that you are looking for a serious relationship. In the United States potential relationship partners are usually found through (1) involvement in groups of people who share our values and interests or (2) introduction by others already in our social support network.
3. Consider signing up for one or more online dating apps (for example, eHarmony, Match, Zoosk, Tinder, etc.). Within the past

decade, these have made it possible to connect with many more potential partners.

4. When meeting someone new, first look for friendship and then for partnership; these are the two most essential elements of a successful long-term relationship. Dramatic romance is more exciting but usually fades. A spirit of casual fun is much more attractive than a sense of neediness.

If you are in a primary relationship that you would like to improve or repair:

1. On a new page or file of your *Record*, list as many functional ideas about your relationship as possible, using the information from this chapter as a guideline.

2. On a new page or file of your *Record*, list the issues about which you and your partner are conflicted and select *just one* to attempt to resolve.

3. Request a meeting to try to resolve that particular conflict. Before the meeting review the "Rules of Fair Fighting" presented earlier and offer them to your partner for review. If violations of a rule occur during the dialogue, review the rule with your partner and seek agreement to pay it greater respect during the remainder of the interaction.

4. On a new page or file of your *Record*, start a list of "My Partner's Best Qualities." Include everything you like—or have ever liked—about them (for example, whatever you found attractive in the past, even if it may seem to have "disappeared" with increased conflict). Add new items whenever possible.

5. On a new page or file of your *Record*, start a list of "Ways to Show Positive Regard." These might include sincere expressions of appreciation, a statement of commitment to the relationship, affectionate notes placed where they will be found, arranging a favorite dining experience, writing a personal poem or letter, completing a long-deferred task, assuming an additional household responsibil-

ity, unexpectedly sending a positive message, or even just sharing your list of "My Partner's Best Qualities."

6. On a new page or file of your *Record*, start a list of "Better Choices," statements or actions that might have been better alternatives than those your partner construed as criticism, blame, threat, or aggression.

7. Propose "responsive listening" for dialogues with your partner about a relationship grievance or complaint. This means that after one person has spoken—and before we express our own point of view—we first attempt to restate what was just said and the feelings that were expressed. Each comment, therefore, begins, "As I understand it, you said . . . and are feeling . . ." Only after the first speaker has confirmed, corrected, or clarified their thoughts and feelings does the second begin presenting their own. This exercise forces participants to listen more carefully to each other and can help each better understand the other's point of view.

8. If emotions become so heated that attempts at dialogue fail, communication is best temporarily restricted to written notes or email to permit careful editing of language that might "trigger" an emotional response or be construed as an attack.

9. If all attempts to resolve problems or conflict via discussion fail, consult a mutually trusted third party or relationship therapist who can serve as referee and consultant.

6

Healthy Relaxation

Prolonged anxiety and tension can damage our health, impair our decision making, and disrupt our sense of well-being. On the other hand, just a two-minute session of relaxation repeated several times each day can relieve the adverse effects of stress, diminish physical pain, and increase lifespan. Developing *calming routines* that soothe anxiety and frustration, therefore, can be crucial to our health—and our peace of mind.

We tend to perform best when we are relaxed. Anxiety can make us hesitant, anger can make us impulsive, and both can cause us to make mistakes and decisions we regret. Whether shooting a basketball, playing an instrument, or solving a mathematical equation, we are most creative and effective when relaxed. When we can detach ourselves from outside distractions and suspend our "inner critic," we are more likely to experience "flow"—a state of intense focus in which all other concerns and distractions fade into "background noise" that is easy to block out. When our focus is on just one task, we perform more smoothly and efficiently, we become more productive and creative, and our sense of well-being is boosted.

STRESS, ANXIETY, AND ANGER

Stress refers to the demands and obstacles we perceive in the outside world. By contrast, *anxiety* and *anger* are internal emotional states we often experience in reaction to stress. Unchecked anxiety or anger can cause adverse health effects (for example, skin outbreaks, headaches, sleep disturbance, etc.), as well as self-defeating levels of irritability or fearfulness. Negative emotional arousal is not, however, an inevitable result of stress. Although we often cannot avoid external stress, we *can* learn to effectively manage our internal emotional state.

Learning to recognize negative emotional arousal in its early stages is important because intense levels are more difficult to manage and can impair our judgment and reasoning. Heightened anxiety or anger temporarily alter the chemistry of our nervous system and cause us to become more self-centered, untrusting, and inconsiderate. Relaxation training teaches us to become more aware (or "mindful") of what we are sensing and feeling. The earlier we intervene with a planned relaxation strategy, the healthier, happier, and more effective we are likely to be.

FUNCTIONAL THOUGHTS THAT CAN CALM US

Shifting greater attention to relevant functional thoughts can prevent negative emotional arousal from reaching harmful proportions. These include ideas such as:

An accepting and understanding attitude can permit me to find a reasonable solution to almost every problem I encounter.

I cannot change, erase, or forget what has already happened—only accept and deal with it.

The quality of my life depends less on what happens to me than how I respond to it.

This will pass and I will feel better again.

Although I cannot control external events or circumstances, I can get better at controlling my internal reactions to them.

Ninety-nine percent of the things I worry about will never come to pass.

Even if my worst fears are realized, I will find a way through.

QUIETING THE LEFT HEMISPHERE

Anxiety and anger are primarily products of the left hemisphere, the area of our brain responsible for language, organization, and acquisitiveness. When the left brain interprets an event or circumstance as "threatening," *cortisol* ("stress hormone") is released into our bloodstream. This causes us to temporarily become emotionally aroused and ready for "fight or flight." When we remain anxious or angry for an extended time, however, elevated levels of cortisol cause prolonged emotional arousal, gradually damaging our internal organ systems. Learning to soothe ourselves and relax can, therefore, be an important step in enhancing our health.

Effective strategies for calming ourselves typically involve quieting our wordy left brain and engaging—and attending more to—our right hemisphere, the "silent" half of our brain that is more responsible for positive and transcendent emotional states like joy and love, as well as our appreciation of art, dance, music, and nature. Standing beside a pristine mountain lake, even when just pictured in our imagination, can inspire relaxation by making everything else seem less important.

Fortunately, our brains also have considerable *neuroplasticity*, the capacity to change and grow. With focused awareness, positive intention, persistent effort, and repeated rehearsal we can gradually overcome and replace even long-standing habits of thought and reaction that have become self-defeating.

MINDFULNESS MEDITATION

Meditation is the act of focusing our attention on just one thing as a way of attaining relaxation or better understanding of ourselves. The term *mindfulness* refers to the nonjudgmental awareness of our experience as it unfolds from moment to moment. Neuroscience research has demonstrated that the practice of *mindfulness meditation* can mitigate anxiety and improve cognitive functioning. Similar research has shown that meditation stimulates the limbic system of the brain to produce more dopamine, the neurotransmitter substance that causes pleasure.

Mindfulness meditation involves (1) purposefully and nonjudgmentally focusing attention on our thoughts and feelings in the immediate moment and (2) attempting to suspend judgment or desire for anything to be different. It means attempting to recognize and experience our internal states without trying to alter them, while expecting nothing more than whatever the present moment brings. We can attain a state of peaceful equanimity if we can peer into our mind and accept whatever we find, letting go of attachment or aversion.

Four basic conditions are usually required for effective meditation:

1. *A quiet environment.* Meditation can take place at home, in a garden or park, at a place of worship, or in any place that is peaceful and pleasant.
2. *A comfortable position.* Best is a position that can be maintained for twenty minutes without inducing sleep, such as sitting or reclining slightly.
3. *An object to dwell on.* This can be a symbolic object that is gazed upon, a repeated sound (for example, God, love, safe, warm, ohm, etc.) or "mantra" (for example, Let it be) that is spoken, or even a sensation or feeling that is made the focus of attention.
4. *A passive, accepting attitude.* Temporarily letting go of concerns, ambitions, and judgments allows thoughts and images to come and go as they will, drifting through our awareness.

A sample protocol designed to induce mindfulness meditation is presented later in this chapter.

FINDING REFUGE IN THE CURRENT MOMENT

The past is what most often makes us sad or angry. The future can inspire our fear and worry. The current moment, on the other hand, often can provide a refuge of peace and calm. Most relaxation methods direct our attention to some aspect of the "here and now," shifting our attention away from past and future sources of distress, relaxing us, and enhancing our peace of mind.

Activity itself can also induce relaxation and diminish muscle tension by forcing us to fully attend to what we are doing in the immediate moment. In the face of major loss or trauma, "throwing" ourselves into activity can sometimes prevent us from becoming overwhelmed and immobilized. In Barbara Kingsolver's novel *The Poisonwood Bible*, a mother who has tragically lost a young daughter describes how nonstop activity helped her cope:

> As long as I kept moving, my grief streamed out behind me like a swimmer's long hair in water. I knew the weight was there but it didn't touch me. Only when I stopped did the slick, dark stuff of it come floating around my face, catching my arms and throat till I began to drown. So I just didn't stop.

Distracting activity can mitigate the effects of pain or sorrow. The more our attention is engaged elsewhere, the less it is available to focus on unpleasant memory or painful sensation.

ONE DAY AT A TIME

The motto of Alcoholics Anonymous, the most respected of the twelve-step self-help recovery programs, is "one day at a time." Looking into the future beyond today can be overwhelming, cause us to feel hopeless, and trigger relapse. Limiting our contemplation of the future (or the past) can help us manage anxiety and preserve peace of mind.

The frontal lobe of our brain permits us to think about the future in a way that other animals cannot. Our ability to devise complex plans for the future is one of the main reasons our species has thrived. Our ability to project ahead in time, however, also permits us to torture ourselves with counterproductive anxiety and worry about the infinite number of potential future calamities.

This "one day at a time" philosophy suggests that we can attain peace of mind if we strive to

1. lead our lives one day (or even one moment) at a time,
2. make the most of each day (or even each moment),
3. let go of regret or remorse about past events,
4. let go of fear and worry about unavoidable events that might happen in the future,
5. view the overcoming of hardship as a pathway to greater self-respect and an expression of love, and
6. accept that life is rarely "fair" but contains the tools we need to overcome the obstacles in our path.

LET IT BE

Like many endeavors in life, success in finding peace of mind can depend on establishing a balance. Although we need to be concerned about potential difficulties so that we can head off trouble, it is also important that we limit our anxiety and worry so that we can function efficiently and enjoy each current moment.

Emotional distress often results from wanting something to be different than it is, and we spend much of our energy trying to influence the world so that our hopes and wishes are fulfilled. No matter how hard we try, and however clever we may be, we are often unsuccessful.

Although refusing to ever "give up" or admit failure may increase the chances we will eventually achieve a goal, that strategy is also likely to result in a great deal of unnecessary frustration. We are perpetually confronted with a tradeoff between our drive to acquire what we want and our wish for contentment. Attaining a balance means that we permit ourselves to abandon the pursuit of goals that may be unattainable or unreasonably costly and let things be as they are. Our peace of mind and emotional well-being can sometimes depend on learning to detach, relax, and accept that which is impossible or unreasonably difficult to change.

Our mental state can benefit from getting better at "letting go" of what is happening "out there" (for example, world events, the actions of others, etc.) and focusing instead on what is going on "in here" (for example, our emotional state, thoughts, tension, etc.). Anxiety that stems from problems beyond our power to resolve—and there are many—is best managed by reducing exertion, accepting that "it is what it is," and finding a way to "go with the flow."

Brain research suggest that our conscious mind—that part of us that we think of as "me"—has less control over our actions than we tend to believe. Instead, subconscious aspects of our mind often determine what we do and our conscious mind then creates an explanation that justifies whatever actions we took. The implication of this surprising finding is that we are usually going to do what our biology and experience have "programmed" us to do. Our peace of mind, therefore, can depend on our ability to accept whatever that might be. Although frequently misguided, we generally do *what seems to be for the best* in the circumstances we encounter. Understanding this can make it easier to forgive ourselves and others—and to retain our emotional composure.

Most of us want to see ourselves as "good." Each of us, however, has objectionable thoughts and feelings we often would rather not acknowledge. Rather than just blotting out our negative aspects and pretending they do not exist, we do better to acknowledge their presence, accept that we cannot control our thoughts and feelings, and control what we can—how we respond.

We also benefit from "letting go" of anger or hate because hanging onto these feelings damages us, not the person whose actions inspired them. Although a desire for justice can tempt us to hang on to resentment, doing so is like taking poison in the hope that someone else will die.

THE "THREE RS" OF EMOTIONAL MANAGEMENT

We often regret decisions we made when we were intensely frightened or angry. We usually make better decisions when our reason is able to predominate our emotions. When we become acutely distressed, therefore, the goal is to *delay*—to postpone action or decision until our emotional arousal has subsided and our rational thought processes can be fully engaged. In the heat of the moment, it can help to recall the "Three Rs" of emotional management:

1. *Refrain.* We can often avoid unwise words or actions we are likely to regret by remaining silent and taking no action at all while our emotions are heated.
2. *Retreat.* Putting distance between ourselves and the source of our negative emotional reaction can improve our perspective and allow us to consider the situation in more rational light.
3. *Rethink.* Once we have calmed down and the frontal cortex of our brain has been reengaged, we become more capable of rationally analyzing the situation and making a wise choice from the available responses.

Employing these three steps can help us make a more thoughtful and constructive assertive response, one we are less likely to regret.

Certain functional thoughts may help to keep us calm during this process, including:

What others do and say reveals much about them and almost nothing about me.

Offensive words and actions usually result from ignorance or emotional damage.

No one can injure me with words alone if I refuse to join them in the effort.

When others go low, I am likely to do better by going high.

Every conflict has potential resolutions that may be impossible to see in the heat of the moment.

WHEN PANIC STRIKES

Sudden and unexplained episodes of intense anxiety are far more frequent than is widely known. Each year approximately one of every one hundred Americans receives professional care for a panic disorder—recurrent, sudden, and unexplained episodes of crippling anxiety—and many times that number suffer attacks but never seek treatment. Panic attacks can include a variety of symptoms but commonly feature feelings of impending doom, rapid heartbeat, shortness of breath, sweating, and chest pain or nausea. Because they can be terrifying and indistinguishable from a life-threatening medical crisis, panic attacks are the leading cause of 911 calls and emergency room visits. After a couple of expensive episodes that result in being told that our symptoms are "just" the result of anxiety, most of us try to manage without medical intervention.

The greatest danger of panic attacks is that we may begin to avoid the places or circumstances in which an episode began—even when there is nothing inherently dangerous about them. This can result in fear of more and more locations and situations, with a corresponding restriction of our movements. The most disabling stage of this process is *agoraphobia*, a state in which we have become so fearful as to become housebound. This crippling state can be prevented if we respond to panic (when there is no identifiable danger) by remaining where we are (or in a comfortable place nearby), reminding ourselves that what we are experiencing is *just another anxiety attack* that won't kill us and will pass, and practicing relaxation techniques such as those presented herein. By refusing to flee, we can diminish the importance of the episode and prevent the place or activity from becoming associated with intense fear.

WHEN TO SEEK PROFESSIONAL HELP

When we continue to feel overwhelmed or immobilized by emotional distress despite our best efforts to calm down, it is probably time to consult a mental health professional. Because physiologic illness sometimes mimics a mental health issue, scheduling an appointment with a primary care physician is often a good first step, especially when energy, concentration, memory, or emotional control are affected. If a physical explanation for our symptoms is ruled out, the physician may be able to recommend a psychologist, psychiatrist, or other licensed psychotherapist. The professionals who fall into the third category vary from state to state but may include clinical social workers, nurse practitioners, and others who have earned a master's degree in a related subject.

Therapists come in many varieties, and finding one with whom we can work well is often more important than the therapist's educational background or clinical orientation. A therapist can help us "shrink" overwhelming and confusing problems into more manageable proportions, prioritize our goals, and identify problem-solving strategies. They can teach us techniques for managing our emotional state and point us in directions more likely to help us respond effectively. They may also be able to help us become aware of the ways in which we inadvertently make our problems worse. Therapists can also provide emotional support and reassurance as we work through a difficult time.

Couples therapy can be particularly helpful when a relationship has become strained. It can be difficult for two individuals who feel injured by each other to work together to resolve conflict. Group therapy is often more affordable and may provide an opportunity to connect with others who are seeking solutions to similar problems.

Severe emotional problems may be related to genetic factors and central nervous system chemistry. In such cases, medications prescribed and monitored by a board certified psychiatrist can be appropriate to restore sufficient emotional control, energy, and motivation to permit us to reasonably manage our lives and avoid the creation of further stressful circumstances.

INDUCING RELAXATION

Several different methods of inducing relaxation have been shown by research to be effective. These include the following.

Deep breathing. Although the primary function of breathing is to oxygenate the blood, slow and rhythmic deep breathing can also quell anxiety and produce a relaxation response. As we encounter stress and tension begins to mount, our breathing automatically quickens and becomes shallower. For this reason, a constructive first response to any emotional upset is to take a few "cleansing" deep breaths. In fact, most forms of meditation begin with a pattern of slow and regular deep breathing, as in the following relaxation induction protocol:

1. Assume a comfortable sitting or reclining position in a quiet place that is free of distractions.
2. With eyes closed and lips pursed (as in blowing out a candle), slowly exhale for as long as possible, imagining as you do that your anxiety, tension, and anger are flowing out with the air being expelled.
3. Once your lungs are empty, pause for a count of ten before beginning to inhale, focusing attention on the constriction of your lungs.
4. Slowly inhale, taking in as much air as possible through your nose and pulling it into the bottom of your lungs (that is, "abdominal breathing").

5. Once your lungs are full, pause for a count of ten before beginning to exhale, focusing attention on the expansion of your lungs.
6. Repeat steps 2 through 5 for five minutes, keeping one hand on your abdomen just below the navel to feel it rise with each inhale and fall with each exhale.
7. Practice this routine three or more times each day and use it whenever heightened tension is noticed.

Progressive Muscle Relaxation. Another method of attaining greater awareness of physical tension—and greater skill at releasing it—is the systematic tension and relaxation of each major muscle group. When following this induction script, stop immediately any procedure that produces pain.

1. Sit back or lie down in a comfortable position, close your eyes, and take a few cleansing deep breaths.
2. Focus your attention on your feet and tense the muscles there by curling your toes and the arch of each foot.
3. Flex the muscles of both feet tightly (but not painfully) for about five seconds, noticing how it feels.
4. Release the tension in your feet, also noticing how that feels.
5. After a pause of about five seconds, again flex, pause, and release the tension in the muscles of your feet, observing the difference in feeling between when they are tense and relaxed.
6. Next move your attention to your lower legs and flex both calf muscles for about five seconds, again noticing how the constriction feels.
7. Flex your leg muscles tightly (but not painfully) for about five seconds, noticing how it feels.
8. Then release the tension of your lower legs, noticing how relaxation feels.
9. After about five seconds, once again flex, pause, and release the tension in the muscles of your lower legs, observing how they feel different when tense and relaxed.

10. Repeat this same pattern of twice tensing and relaxing (and no-
    ticing the difference in feeling) the muscles of your
    a. upper legs and pelvis (by tightly squeezing your thighs
       together),
    b. stomach and chest (by sucking your stomach in),
    c. back (by bringing your shoulders together behind you),
    d. arms and hands (by making fists and squeezing all the way up
       your arm),
    e. neck and head (by tensing the muscles around your neck,
       mouth, and eyes), and finally
    f. entire body (by flexing the muscles of your feet, legs, stomach,
       chest, arms, shoulders, neck, and head all at the same time).
11. Slowly "wake up" your body by stirring your muscles and adjust-
    ing your arms and legs.
12. When feeling ready, stretch your muscles and open your eyes.

Mindfulness Meditation. Six to eight weeks of daily twelve-minute
sessions of practicing the steps listed here will usually lead to effective meditation, although many experts recommend thirty minutes of
practice for the first two weeks. Start by selecting a focus of attention,
such as a symbolic object or picture, a chanted "mantra" (a sound like
"ohm," a word like "warm" or "safe," or a phrase like "let it be"), or
just your uncontrolled passing thoughts, feelings, or sensations. Then
employ the following steps:

1. Relax yourself by using the deep breathing induction protocol
   presented earlier.
2. Focus as much of your attention as possible on your predeter-
   mined object or subject.
3. Each time you become distracted—a common occurrence—
   simply and nonjudgmentally return the focus of your conscious
   awareness to your breath.
4. Attempt to "let go" of all desires and concerns and become a passive and accepting observer, suspending negative judgments and
   assuming that everything is as it should be.

5. Notice—and attempt to savor—any observations that inspire a sense of gratitude.
6. Try to make time meaningless.
7. Attempt to suspend certainty about anything and understand that everyone's view of reality is often inaccurate.

An Inventory of the Senses. Another way to escape thoughts of the past and future, become more grounded in the current moment, and attain greater relaxation is to conduct "an inventory of the senses." This is accomplished by first focusing attention on, and naming to ourselves, everything we see. The focus of attention is then shifted to everything we hear, which we also silently name. Our attention is subsequently refocused onto—and we name—everything we smell, taste, and feel on our skin, respectively.

Visual Imagery. Our imagination can also transport us to a setting that relaxes or inspires us. This may be different for each of us and the goal is to find what works best for us. The process takes only a minute or two but can be employed intermittently in many different circumstances. What follows is a sample visualization protocol designed to induce relaxation:

> Get comfortable, close your eyes, and take a deep cleansing breath. Now imagine that you are comfortably reclining on a tropical hillside overlooking the ocean. Notice the beautiful colors, the many different greens of the dense foliage, the blues of the ocean, the sparkling white sand beach, the multicolored wildflowers scattered over the hillside. Notice the sounds of the ocean waves pounding the rocks and beach of the coastline, the bird songs, and gentle breeze passing through the trees. Notice the natural smells of the ocean and plants. Notice the feeling on your skin of the warm sun and gentle ocean breeze that cools you to the perfect temperature. Notice that everything is just as it should be and all tension and discomfort is drifting away from your body.

Activity Inductions. Choreographed patterns of movement can also induce relaxation by focusing our attention on what we are doing in the moment and drawing us out of that part of our mind responsible for anxiety and worry. Such techniques include yoga, tai chi, and even the traditional Japanese tea ceremony. More esoteric methods, such as "tapping touch"—using our fingertips to lightly tap ourselves from foot to head—have also been shown to serve as effective relaxation techniques.

Countless activities can induce relaxation, although their effectiveness can vary from person to person. Any involvement can be calming if it takes us "out of our head" and focuses our attention away from thoughts that inspire tension. This is one of the reasons that hobbies are so popular (and healthy). When our hands and eyes are occupied in attempting to accomplish a task, our troubles shift into the background, reality becomes less disturbing, and we become more relaxed.

Guided Relaxation Induction. In conjunction with the deep breathing or progressive muscle relaxation inductions presented earlier (or both), the script presented here is designed to induce a state of optimal relaxation and positive feeling. It should be recorded so that it can be employed whenever anxiety begins to disrupt our peace of mind. (Although there may be some who are not helped by this type of exercise, the risk of harm is minimal; personal control is retained while awake, and if sleep occurs the result is no more harmful than would be taking a nap.)

Begin by making a recording of either the "deep breathing" or "progressive muscle relaxation" induction protocol presented earlier, whichever works better for you. If both protocols prove effective, they can be combined by first recording the deep breathing then recording the muscle relaxation induction. Then add the following directions to your recording:

Create this picture in your mind's eye:

You're walking along a beautiful beach, noticing that the water is pristine and the sand is extremely white and fine. Feel the ocean mist gently cooling the warmth of the sun on your skin. Now you come to a magical garden that is green and lush and beautiful. Take a moment to see the vivid colors of the flowers and hear the melodies of the songbirds. It is so beautiful and peaceful here. This garden is the most serene and tranquil place you've ever been.

As you float through the magical garden you come to a small building with a set of spectacular elevator doors made of rich mahogany with lavish gold trim. These elevator doors are as beautiful as everything else around you. Now you see that the doors have opened and you step inside, knowing that the elevator will take you down to your own special place of peace and security, a room where no one else can go and where you can be completely safe and entirely comfortable.

The elevator lights reveal that you are on the tenth floor. You push the button marked one, and the elevator begins to descend toward your special room of comfort on the bottom floor. As you pass each floor on your way down you become more and more relaxed, more and more peaceful. You're going down, deeper and deeper. You pass the ninth floor, now the eighth floor, now the seventh. You're going deeper and deeper, feeling more and more serene and comfortable the further you descend. The sixth floor goes by. Then you pass five, four, three, two. At last you reach floor number one. The doors open and you step out into your special enchanted room. You're finally here, in your perfect place of safety and comfort, perfectly relaxed and perfectly at peace.

Now you enter your own special room where you sit down in the most comfortable chair in the world, the one that is waiting there for you. Feel yourself melting into the chair, like a pat of butter slowly softening in the sun. No sizzle, just slow, slow melting. That's you melting into your chair, becoming completely relaxed and completely at peace. And it's a great comfort to realize that you can return to this place (and this feeling) whenever the cares of the world begin to cause you to feel stressed or anxious.

Relaxation is most easily attained in a safe and quiet location. Once a technique has been learned well, however, it can be used as many times, in as many circumstances, and on as many occasions as helps us increase relaxation and enhance our peace of mind.

STEPS TOWARD RELAXATION

1. Record in your *Record of Functional Thought* as many ideas as you can find that motivate you to improve your relaxation skills, using this chapter as a guide.

2. Try out each of the relaxation techniques presented in this chapter to determine which work best for you and list those in your *Record*.

3. Make recordings of the relaxation induction protocols that work best for you and list them in your *Record*.

4. Whenever you experience heightened anxiety or tension, employ one of the relaxation techniques or recorded relaxation inductions you listed in your *Record*.

5. Whenever you experience frustration or anger, attempt to employ the "Three Rs of Anger Management" presented earlier in this chapter.

7

In Pursuit of Well-Being

Health is the foundation on which we build our lives. Irrespective of religious belief, our body is best thought of as a "temple," the structure on which our ability to accomplish almost everything is based. Whether Olympic-class athlete or quadriplegic, the better we nurture ourselves and attend to our physical well-being, the more likely we are to feel—and be—capable of attaining our goals and overcoming the insults and challenges of life.

Medical research has shown—and almost all of us know—that we are likely to be healthier, happier, smarter, and live longer by:

1. Not smoking.
2. Maintaining a healthy weight.
3. Being active.
4. Eating more fruit, vegetables, nuts, whole grains, and fish and less red meat and animal fat.
5. Drinking alcohol only in moderation.
6. Working with a health care provider to monitor our health and identify and manage any medical problems we might develop.

Despite knowing that following these recommendations would improve our health, many of us fail to consistently adopt them, often because

1. dysfunctional thoughts destroy our motivation and prevent or detract from our efforts to improve our health habits, and/or
2. the short-term rewards of unhealthy behavior often influence our actions more than the potential future benefits of healthier actions.

We can overcome both of these obstacles, however, by (1) learning to focus on thoughts that inspire healthier actions and (2) better understanding—and utilizing—the factors that most control our health-related choices.

LEARNING TO CREATE
THE ILLUSION OF WILLPOWER

Many of us mistakenly doubt our capacity to alter unhealthy patterns of behaviors because we wrongly believe that we lack a character trait called "willpower" or "self-discipline." Most of us have failed at attempts to exercise more, eat healthier, drink less, quit smoking, or alter some other self-defeating habit, and these failures have solidified the idea that we possess some fault that makes us incapable of succeeding. And when this type of dysfunctional thought becomes the focus of our attention, our motivation to even attempt change can disintegrate. As a result, we miss the opportunities to improve our health-related behavior patterns—and whatever physical, cognitive, and emotional benefits they might produce.

Research has shown that the ability to delay gratification—to sacrifice an immediate reward to obtain a more important one later—is *more learned than inherent.* In other words, accomplishing long-term goals such as adopting healthier habits depends more on finding sufficient motivation and the right strategy than on any character trait we might be born with or without. The terms "willpower" and "self-discipline" are simply descriptions we assign to individuals who have *learned* how to (1) generate sufficient motivation and (2) implement an effective strategy.

Both research and experience have found that simply exerting "self-control" can be a successful short-term strategy for delaying gratification or tolerating unpleasantness but that it almost never succeeds in the long run. In Alcoholics Anonymous this practice is referred to as "white knuckling" and is considered a sign of resistance to the program that can achieve long-term sobriety.

FUNCTIONAL THOUGHTS
THAT CAN MOTIVATE HABIT CHANGE

We can inspire greater hope of success and increase our motivation to pursue constructive action by focusing on functional thoughts about adopting healthier habits. Such thoughts include:

Each time I can adopt a healthier habit I am likely to improve my physical, cognitive, and emotional well-being.

Only I can improve my health habits, and I can learn everything required to make those changes.

Taking better care of myself will allow me to be more nearly what I want to be as a spouse, partner, child, parent, sibling, friend, worker, community member, and citizen.

By striving to change one habit at a time, setting easily attained goals, valuing slow incremental changes, and persisting in the face of seeming "failure," I will eventually establish healthier habits.

By making healthier routines easily available and more pleasant I can increase their frequency.

Rewarding health-promoting activity can increase my motivation and my chances of making positive habit change.

If I refuse to give up, persist at trying to do better, and continue paying attention to my health, I can't fail to eventually improve my health-related habits.

Adopting healthier habits is my best hope of improving whatever health issues I hope to change.

STRATEGIES FOR SUCCESS

Assuming we have found sufficient motivation, success at improving our health-related habits depends on finding strategies that will enhance our ability to delay gratification. Successful strategies for delaying gratification have been found to often include the following features:

1. Tackling just one issue at a time.
2. Setting incremental behavior goals (that is, each small step I hope to accomplish on the path to my long-term goal).
3. Creating a "calendar" of incremental goals—the steps we hope to accomplish—and checking each off as it is reached (or, if not reached, adding more easily reached intermediate steps).
4. Sharing goals and plans with supportive others.
5. Acknowledging the frustration involved in deferring gratification and finding "offsets," healthier forms of gratification that can provide at least partial compensation for the short-term gratification we have given up to pursue our long-term goal.
6. Frequently reviewing our plan and making adjustments to compensate for "slip-ups" and setbacks.
7. Noting and celebrating every positive step accomplished—no matter how small—toward our goal and sharing each with supportive others.
8. Noting the positive feeling associated with attempting healthy change.

When we wrongly attribute our failure to improve unhealthy behavior patterns to the absence or lack of some internal quality or characteristic, we create the illusion that success is impossible and our incentive to persist diminishes. Any of us is capable of improving our health routines by finding sufficient motivation and implementing a reasonable strategy—and in doing so we can create an illusion of "willpower."

ADOPTING HEALTHIER ROUTINES

If we hope to improve our health, our best goal is to adopt *healthier habits*. Programs that have been found to produce lasting improvements in health habits also include the following features:

1. *Medical consultation.*
   In addition to ensuring our fitness to change our exercise and diet habits, a primary care physician may be able to provide supportive treatment and guidance.
2. *A focus on changing one routine at a time.*
   Attempting to change more than one health routine at a time should be avoided because of the added opportunity for frustration.
3. *Easily attained goals specified in terms of behavior, not health status.*
   Thirty minutes of walking or eating five carrot slices before any other snack are better goals than losing ten pounds or lowering blood pressure twenty points.
4. *A "success friendly" environment.*
   We can reduce the "friction" that makes it difficult to develop an exercise habit by making sure that appropriate clothing and equipment are readily accessible and that we have options for increasing our level of activity. If we hope to develop healthier eating habits, we can collect a stockpile of healthy choices and dispose of unhealthy options.

5. *One or more health habit change partners.*

   Sharing mutual support with someone else who is striving for similar goals can increase the pleasure of the activity and boost motivation.

6. *Pairing or rewarding healthy behavior with preferred activities.*

   For example, watching a football game or TV show or chatting while peddling a stationary bike can make the activity more attractive. Healthy eating can be made more pleasurable by finding recipes for tasty meals that contain healthy ingredients and by planning a pleasurable activity (a hot bath, time with a friend, playing a video game, etc.) as a reward.

7. *"Setbacks" or "failure" are only signals that the plan may need to be adjusted.*

   Establishing healthier routines often requires tolerance for events that might seem like failure. We are all human and far from perfect. We inevitably encounter days when the obstacles will prevail. We sometimes succumb to temptations such as taking a nap instead of exercising or eating rich foods (or amounts of food) that we had intended to avoid. Rather than representing "failure," experiences of this type are entirely *normal* and almost unavoidable. They are meaningful only if our focus stalls on a dysfunctional interpretation, we abandon our self-improvement efforts, and we begin ignoring our health-related behavior. If we can instead forgive ourselves for being human, adjust our plan to establish healthier habits, and continue to pay attention to our health-related routines, we will eventually succeed.

   "Failure" becomes close to impossible if we define success as perseverance and flexibility—adjusting rather than giving up or turning attention away from the issue of improving health-related routines. By being flexible and adjusting our plans when we encounter frustration, we give ourselves the best chance of shaping our behavior in the direction we desire. If we keep adjusting—rather than abandoning—our efforts, we can eventually establish an effective exercise habit.

8. *Avoiding deprivation.*

Allowing ourselves to become too tired, hungry, thirsty, sleep deprived, lonely, socially committed, or stressed can overtax our internal resources and impair our self-control. Remembering to eat, rest, or talk with a friend can prevent the type of "ego depletion" and make moderation—in which everything is permissible—more probable.

Developing an exercise routine provides a good example of how we can create an illusion of self-discipline. Those of us who have established a consistent exercise routine—and created an illusion of willpower or self-discipline as a result—have succeeded by reducing the negative expectation and anticipated difficulty that create reluctance (the "friction") and increasing the short-term payoffs of performing the activity (the "reward"). Rather than possessing some unique inner strength, we have simply found a way to tip the motivational balance toward the desired outcome, the establishment of an exercise routine. All of us are capable of establishing more healthful behavior patterns if we (1) increase our awareness that success is possible and (2) implement a sensible strategy based on what science has learned about changing habits.

DEVELOPING AN EXERCISE ROUTINE

When a good friend asked his cardiologist how he could prevent his accumulated arterial blockage from causing a stroke or heart attack, the doctor's response was, "It's hard to hit a moving target." What he was suggesting is that *being active is vital to good health* and movement becomes more important as our health risks increase. Although prescribed medications, rest, diet, personal relationships, and challenging mental activity are also important, our well-being often depends on frequent physical activity. In fact, a regular exercise routine has been found to be as close to a "magic pill" for improving our health as exists.

Apart from taking medications as prescribed and receiving appropriate medical treatment, we are most likely to enhance our health by (1) establishing an exercise routine and (2) adopting healthier eating habits. And the former (establishing an exercise routine) usually holds the greatest promise of enhancing our health. Regular exercise has been shown to improve health, increase life span, brighten mood, help manage insomnia and pain, increase energy, and even prevent or delay dementia.

Despite its documented benefits, establishing a regular exercise routine can be a difficult proposition. Inertia, the tendency to continue our usual patterns of behavior, can be a difficult obstacle to overcome. We can sometimes find motivation in the wishes of loved ones—or in the memory of someone we have lost—who would want us to live healthier and longer lives.

We can also improve our chances of establishing an exercise habit by selecting an activity that is readily available and suited to our physical condition, circumstances, and preferences—in other words, one that we would be likely to perform. If other forms of exercise also meet these criteria, alternating activities from day to day can enhance interest and allow the specific muscle groups more time to recuperate.

Walking is a good exercise option for many of us because it requires little preparation or equipment. Running burns calories faster, but can take a greater toll on feet, knees, and backs. If available, exercise machines (for example, elliptical trainers, stair-steppers, stationary bicycles, rowing machines, strength building resistance devices, etc.) can be easier on our joints and may be more suited to those of us with physical impairments. Bicycling can be an enjoyable exercise activity, but the equipment involved can be expensive and the potential benefits may be outweighed by the risks of riding in automobile traffic. When a pool is available, swimming or water aerobics can offer low-trauma exercise, as well as potential for secondary social pleasure. Depending on season and location, the pleasure involved in activities such as skating, hiking, skiing (downhill or cross country), canoeing, and kayaking can be reinforcing while providing the benefits of exercise.

When a pool is available, simply treading water can be good exercise for the entire body. Exercises that can be performed at home are often most convenient. Although possibly more tedious, walking up and down steps at home or work (or even just repeatedly stepping up and down on one step) can produce as much exercise benefit as using a stair-stepper machine. It is even possible to exercise while reclining on a bed: alternately lifting and bending the left knee and right arm and then the right knee and left arm ("marching in place on your back").

Stretching before and after exercise can reduce the risk of injury and enhance flexibility. Applying heat immediately prior to exercise can also help to loosen up muscles and joints, whereas applying cold immediately after finishing can minimize inflammation.

Although there are many options for attempting to start an exercise program, one recommended strategy is to dedicate thirty minutes of each day with the goal of eventually being able to perform a selected exercise activity continuously for the entire time. The next step is to see if we can perform the exercise for sixty seconds every five minutes for the thirty minutes. When we are unable to complete six minutes of exercise in a thirty-minute period, a lighter exercise activity is probably indicated.

Focusing on duration rather than intensity usually works best. If the exercise activity can be performed continuously for six of the thirty dedicated minutes, the goal becomes to gradually increase the percentage of the thirty minutes that we are engaging in the activity (for example, possibly to six ninety-second sessions with 4.5-minute rest intervals). Our goal is to incrementally expand the time we are actively exercising during the dedicated thirty minutes. By giving ourselves permission to rest—or even cut back on our expectation—when we encounter pain, shortness of breath, or discouragement, we can eventually reach the long-term goal, thirty minutes of continuous exercise.

Although thirty minutes of exercise most days of the week will provide most of the benefits of exercise, after reaching that milestone those of us who wish to burn more calories or build greater stamina or strength can gradually pursue even greater duration and/or effort intensity. Other forms of exercise activity (for example, yoga, weight training, specific physical therapies, etc.) might also be added to pursue targeted goals.

An exercise routine can produce benefits that are self-sustaining, but usually only after it has become well established. Once we are accustomed to regular exercise, we often begin to experience short-term reward due to the pleasure associated with being able to perform the exercise activity well and the mild euphoria that sometimes occurs upon completion of an exercise routine. If we persist, our exercise routine is also likely to be reinforced by physical and physiologic benefits (such as improved energy, strength, endurance, weight control, heart rate, blood sugar, or even blood pressure). During approximately the first six weeks of a new exercise routine, however, it can be crucial to find other sources of pleasure to associate with it to provide short-term reinforcement.

ALTERING EATING HABITS

Because our eating behavior has a strong emotional component, most of us have trouble following prescribed diets and only rarely do they have long-term success. The more restrictive a diet, the less likely it is to become part of our routine. For most of us a simpler and more flexible approach to improving our eating habits is likely to have better results.

Almost any diet plan would produce weight loss *if we could follow it indefinitely*. Our best goal, therefore, is to establish healthier eating habits that we can make part of our daily routine. Rather than being restrictive, the best diet programs strive to create a balance that can be sustained. No food needs to be forbidden so long as we have a healthy means of compensating for what we eat by consuming fewer—or burning more—calories at another time.

Efforts to change our eating habits tend to be more successful when they involve keeping a daily food diary, limiting fat consumption, eating more slowly, delaying second helpings and dessert, making a commitment to a partner, stocking up on nutritious and low-calorie foods (for example, carrots, celery, other vegetables, pickles, unbuttered popcorn, pretzels, low-calorie crackers, hummus, and fruit), eating more in the early part of the day and less in the evenings, keeping ourselves satisfied, remembering that "fresh is best," eating everything but in moderation, tolerating "slip-ups," and staying off the scale. We can only control our actions, not our weight or waist measurement.

Research has shown that a simple program of recording each night (1) the food we have eaten and (2) all our calorie-burning activity is just as effective at long-term weight loss as even the most expensive diet programs. Like all behavioral change programs, the key to long-term success is our ability to persevere. Just knowing that later in the day we will be recording our food intake and exercise output can cause us to consume fewer—and expend more—calories.

MANAGING SELF-DEFEATING COMPULSIONS

Nearly 25 percent of Americans report at least monthly abuse of alcohol, almost 10 percent report current use of illicit drugs, and many others experience major life disruption due to behavioral addictions to eating, sex, shopping, video games, or social media. The Surgeon General estimates the costs resulting from substance abuse alone at approximately $450 billion each year. The toll of self-destructive compulsive behavior on families and individuals is tragic. Not only can self-defeating habits be physically harmful and impair a person's ability to solve problems and make positive strides, but they also result in a self-preoccupation that drives a wedge between the individual involved and everyone else.

A major obstacle to the management of substance abuse is *psychological denial.* Until a catastrophic consequence is encountered, those of us who misuse alcohol or drugs tend to feel that our biggest problem is that others are critical of our attempt to relieve stress and have a little pleasure. Nevertheless, professional consultation is recommended for anyone who has experienced one of the following:

1. Had the thought or been told that we should stop or reduce our use of a substance.
2. Become annoyed at someone because they criticized our use.
3. Felt bad or guilty about using.
4. Used in the morning to steady nerves or ease the effects of prior use.

Until the recent introduction of medications that block alcohol or drug receptor neurons, medical science had little to offer abusers of alcohol or drugs. Twelve-step self-help programs like Alcoholics Anonymous and Narcotics Anonymous represented the best hope of recovery, even though fewer than 15 percent of initial attendees achieve uninterrupted long-lasting sobriety and relapses are common. Prescription medications are now available that can prevent intoxication and eliminate motivation to use, but they are only effective when consistently taken. Unfortunately, chronic substance users sometimes discontinue medication and use again because they feel "okay" or "decent" only while under the influence. *Treating substance abuse with receptor-blocking medications has proven more effective than involvement in a twelve-step program alone, but the best treatment approach is to combine the two.*

Although no medications have been found to be effective for the treatment of "behavioral addictions" (for example, compulsive gambling, eating, sex, video game playing, etc.), professional mental health treatment combined with a twelve-step self-help recovery program (for example, Gamblers Anonymous, Overeaters Anonymous, Anorexics and Bulimics Anonymous, Sex Addicts Anonymous, etc.) has helped many.

GIVING UP TOBACCO

We all know by now that smoking is bad for our health and most of us who smoke want to stop. Addiction to nicotine can be strong, however, and quitting cigarettes usually takes both a powerful commitment and careful planning.

Although there is no one "right" way to stop smoking, finding the methods and timing that match our individual needs is often critical to success. It is important to remember that relapsing is not an indication of moral weakness or lack of willpower. It simply means that we have not yet found the right inspiration and techniques.

A good first step is to collect enough information that we can make a plan suited to our circumstances. A good information resource is "QuitAssist," a program that provides a wealth of information about smoking cessation programs, telephone quit lines, websites, guides, and expert information. The federal government has also published the "You Can Quit Smoking Consumer Guide," which can be ordered at 1-800-358-9295 or found on the Surgeon General's website (www. surgeongeneral.gov/tobacco/quits.htm).

Research has shown that combining strategies improves our chances of becoming smoke free. The most effective smoking cessation programs have been found to include the following steps:

1. *Getting ready.* Choose a specific date to stop—perhaps a birthday or anniversary—and mark it on the calendar. Prepare by attempting to reduce stress and learn relaxation techniques. A daily review of a list of all the ways that quitting smoking will improve our life and health can add to our motivation. We can also get rid of cigarettes and ashtrays and other reminders of smoking and plan to avoid others who might encourage smoking.

2. *Seeking support and encouragement.* The more people who know about our attempt to stop smoking, the better its chances for success. Tell everyone we know why and how we plan to stop. We can also ask the people who want us to stop smoking the most to write encouraging notes that we can post in the places we would most be tempted to smoke (for example, on the coffeemaker, above the TV, on the dashboard of our car, etc.). It is entirely appropriate to ask others not to smoke in our presence and to keep their ciga-

rettes out of sight. Support and tips may be available from people we know who have successfully quit. Finally, we may be able to get involved in a stop smoking program at a local health facility.

3. *Acquiring quitting skills.* Quitting smoking may best be considered a skill, like riding a bicycle. It requires figuring out how to move forward, maintaining balance, and persisting if a setback occurs. Write down plans for dealing with symptoms and cravings (for example, a friend to call, a quick walk to take, nicotine gum or lozenges, juices, sugarless gum, hard candy, etc.). We can also have something available that we can hold in the hand that held a cigarette (for example, a pencil, pen, or stress ball, etc.) or that we can place in our mouth (for example, carrot sticks, popcorn, candy, etc.). We can make a list of alternative fun activities (for example, a hot bath, getting massage, watching a favorite recorded TV show, etc.) that we can use to reward nonsmoking. We can be prepared to manage the sleep disturbance and GI disruption that often occur during the first week or two of withdrawal from nicotine by limiting caffeine after noon and eating more raw fruits and vegetables or high-fiber cereal. A class on relaxation techniques or meditation or tai chi can also be helpful.

4. *Consulting a doctor about medications that might help.* Both bupropion (Zyban and Wellbutrin) and varenicline (Chantix) have been shown to reduce cravings for cigarettes.

COPING WITH INSOMNIA

We require sufficient sleep to function at our best. Sleep researchers have discovered that the closer we come to obtaining seven to eight hours of sleep each night, the sharper our thinking and memory, the less likely we are to develop serious illnesses, the quicker and more complete our recovery from serious injury or illness, and the longer we are likely to live. And trying to "catch up" for sleep lost during the week by sleeping longer on the weekend has been shown to be of only limited help. In other words, it should be our goal to get as close to eight hours of sleep each night as possible and to find ways to cope when we sleep less.

Unfortunately, sedatives—medications that can induce a sleep-like state—can prevent the healthy sleep rhythm necessary to reap the full benefits of sleeping. This means that the adverse side effects of both alcohol and sleep aid medications like Ambien may outweigh the benefit of whatever added sleep they provide. Hormonal treatments like melatonin have been shown to make it easier to sleep at an unusual hour but to be less effective at inducing sleep at bedtime.

A combination of over-the-counter sleep aids and behavioral adjustments or "sleep hygiene" represents our best chance of increasing the benefits we obtain from sleep. Those of us who feel alert and awake late at night but function less well early in the morning are classified as "night owls." Those of us who experience the reverse (difficulty staying up late and alertness in the morning) are called "larks." In either case, it can be important to adjust our work or school schedule when possible so that we can sleep and function during the hours most natural for us. Many of us who are by nature "night owls" have been unfairly labeled "lazy" or "irresponsible" because of our difficulty functioning in the early morning. From a biological perspective it would make sense for schools and employers to provide schedules that fit both patterns of alertness.

Insomnia can be mitigated by developing a regular bedtime routine and engaging in some form of daily exercise. Specific recommendations that may help include:

1. *Establish specific sleep and waking hours.* Our bodies gradually become accustomed and conform to whatever schedule we impose.
2. *Avoid napping during the day.* Thirty to forty-five minutes of afternoon napping have been shown to be healthful for those of us who are sleeping well at night but to exacerbate a sleep disturbance.

3. *Avoid caffeine, alcohol, or spicy or heavy foods during the five hours immediately prior to sleep.*
4. *Exercise most days or every day, but not within the last two hours before sleep.*
5. *Eliminate as much noise and light from your bedroom as possible (or consider use of earplugs and/or sleeping mask).*
6. *Reserve the bed for sleep (and sex).* The greater the percentage of your time in bed that you are sleeping, the more your body associates the two.
7. *About thirty minutes before bedtime, eat a light snack of milk or foods high in tryptophan (for example, bananas), which can help induce sleep.*
8. *Establish a presleep ritual, such as a warm bath or a few minutes of reading.*
9. *Practice a relaxation technique just before bedtime.*
10. *Avoid use of electronic screens during the last thirty minutes before bedtime.*
11. *If still awake thirty minutes after attempting to sleep, it can help to get up, go to another room, and read (from a nonelectronic book or magazine) until sleepy.*

STEPS TOWARD WELL-BEING

1. Record in your *Record of Functional Thought* as many functional thoughts about improving your health habits as possible, using the ideas presented in this chapter as a guide.
2. Review the functional thoughts you have listed with one or more trusted others (for example, close friend, sibling, mentor, therapist, spouse, etc.) and modify it and add functional thoughts based on their input.
3. Review the list at least once each day until your health habit goals have been attained.

4. If you suspect—or have been told—that you should reduce your drinking, drug use, or some other compulsive self-defeating behavior, consult a physician about the advisability of a trial of prescription medication, professional behavioral health consultation, and/or becoming involved in a twelve-step recovery program.

5. Before implementing any plan to improve a health habit, consult your primary care physician to rule out any medical condition that might restrict your efforts and to inquire about potential medical treatment that might aid them.

6. Select *just one* health-related routine to change first. Unless necessary for medical reasons, additional changes are best delayed until the first has either been accomplished and maintained for six weeks or has been discarded as unrealistic. Steps 5 through 13 should then be followed for each subsequent habit change goal.

7. Try to find a "change partner," someone with whom you can share goals, motivation, efforts, progress, setbacks, and encouragement to persist.

8. Set an initial goal that is easy to reach. Specify the goal in terms of *habits you hope to establish* rather than how you would like your body or health to change (for example, walking for thirty minutes most days or eating healthier snacks, not losing weight or lowering blood pressure).

9. Obtain whatever is needed to implement the plan. For example, if your goal is to establish an exercise routine, make sure to have appropriate shoes, clothing, space, and equipment. If your goal is to establish healthier eating habits, obtain plenty of nutritious low-calorie foods such as celery, carrots, apples, berries, hummus, and pretzel chips.

10. Make your healthy goal behavior as rewarding as possible. Combine it with pleasant activity such as chatting, watching TV, or listening to music. Reward success with a preferred activity.

11. Focus on duration and perseverance rather than intensity and perfect compliance. Begin at an easy pace and with minimal

resistance. Give yourself permission to change goals when your efforts become unpleasant or discouraging.

12. List in your *Record* all healthy behavior (for example, minutes of exercise activity, healthy foods consumed, etc.) engaged in each day.

13. Remember that "slip-ups" are normal and unavoidable, frustration is a signal that it is time to change goals and/or tactics, and success is guaranteed if we refuse to give up.

8

Defining Our Goals

The key to being successful lies in how we define the goals we hope to accomplish. Although the word "success" often triggers images of great wealth or fame, neither has proven a consistent predictor of happiness or peace of mind. Although basic financial security can be crucial to finding contentment, either great wealth or fame can create more problems than it solves. Although acquiring affluence or celebrity might be initially thrilling, both often drive a wedge between ourselves and others and can cause us to become suspicious of other people's motives. It can reasonably be argued that "peace of mind" is the best measure of "success." After all, what more could we reasonably hope to achieve?

IN SEARCH OF MEANING

Among our greatest challenges is finding a sense of purpose. We find meaning in different ways: religious faith, family connections, personal relationships, community involvement, political activity, career or business achievement, artistic expression, volunteer work, humanitarian service, creative hobbies, and more. Devoting ourselves to a cause we believe in can enhance our sense of purpose. This might be nurturing a child, helping others in need, promoting racial or ethnic awareness or justice, assisting victims of violence or persecution, seeking humane treatment for animals, creating objects of beauty or practical use, or saving the environment. Investing our time and energy in a cause we find worthwhile adds meaning to our lives. Combining several sources of involvement can create an even stronger sense of belonging and completeness.

Our families, neighborhoods, and communities often provide opportunities to develop new—or improve existing—relationships, become involved in good works and charitable endeavors, and/or join groups of people with similar interests or attitudes. The website meetup.com provides information about every organization meeting in each zip code, as well as details on how to get involved. The Internet provides innumerable means of interacting with others, acquiring knowledge, and/or entertaining ourselves. Our opportunities to find connection and meaning in life are almost unlimited.

Many smaller "worlds" exist within our larger one and becoming involved in one or more of these can provide a healthy sense of connection and diversion. For example, there are "worlds" of classic automobiles, bicycle tours, quilting, cribbage tournaments, ham radio communication, etc. There are many "worlds" of potential interest of which we are unaware, awaiting our discovery. Repeatedly shifting the focus of our attention to functional thoughts that inspire hope and constructive action can be the key that motivates us sufficiently to seek out and take advantage of these opportunities.

The people of Denmark, who every year are found to be among the happiest people on Earth, place great value on what they call *hygge* ("hoo-guh"), which translates roughly as "cozying up." Danes take pride in comforting and consoling each other and downplay competition and the acquisition of wealth or nonessential possessions. This people-oriented perspective appears to account for their high rate of satisfaction with life. We also may find greater peace and contentment by emphasizing these values.

The days of our lives are a limited precious resource, and we all hope to spend them as wisely as possible. As we near the end of life, we usually find our time spent with loved ones to be most meaningful. We evolved as social animals and most of us thrive best when we feel emersed in a community of family members, friends, acquaintances, neighbors, and fellow citizens. Isolation is usually incompatible with peace of mind, and we almost always have opportunities to reach out to others in a loving, repentant, or forgiving manner. And in this way, we may be able to improve a relationship or even restore one that has been lost.

WANTING WHAT WE HAVE

A popular bumper sticker pronounces that "He who dies with the most toys wins!" Assuming we can afford them, collecting and enjoying possessions can be a healthy diversion. Few of us, however, find either material possessions or money alone to infuse life with great meaning or quality. Appreciating whatever is positive about our life is far more likely to evoke feelings of contentment and peace of mind. The lyrics of a Sheryl Crow hit song communicate this message well:

> I don't have digital.
> I don't have diddly squat.
> It's not having what you want,
> It's wanting what you have.

The uncharitable among us sometimes portray those who have not been financially successful as "losers." No one is a loser, however, who treats others with respect, refuses to give up on life, and attempts to share loving feelings with others. Anyone who labels others as "losers" has revealed a serious corruption of character that would limit their capacity to develop loving relationships.

BALANCING OUR THOUGHTS

None of us can fully "know" the true nature of the reality that sur-
rounds us. We rely instead on an incomplete and often inaccurate model
constructed by the left hemisphere of our brain. When that imperfect
model leads to a distressing view of an event, the best remedy is often
to challenge the model and find a more positive alternative perspective.

Whereas left hemisphere thinking causes us to see others as competitors or objects to manipulate, the right hemisphere allows us to see our
similarities, how strangers are like our sibling, parent, or child. Whereas
the right brain might want us to "do unto others as we would have
them do unto us," the left brain wants us to do unto others *before* they
do unto us.

Although both aspects of this dichotomy are essential for successful
living, a shift in balance toward the left hemisphere can result in po-
larization or even violent conflict. When ruled by the left hemisphere
people can come to see their adversaries as less than human, creating
the potential for acts of great evil, as occurred in Nazi Germany and
Rwanda. The left brain tends to divide and separate us; the right brain
tends to bring us closer together.

Although it is easy to become preoccupied with our left brain desires
for material possessions and control, we are far more likely to enhance
our peace of mind by focusing our attention on right brain motives,
such as empathy, comradery, and appreciation of art and humor. Activities that involve right brain concerns—such as art, music, dance,
family, friends, community, spirituality, literature, philosophy, charity,
etc.—are more likely to result in a peaceful world and a greater sense
of meaning.

RELATIVITY AND HUMILITY

Everything in our lives is relative. Whether we feel rich or poor depends
on where we stand with respect to the past and within our commu-

nity. If we have just suffered a financial setback or discovered that our neighbors are better off, we tend to feel poor. On the other hand, if our wealth has recently grown or we learn that we are more affluent than others, we tend to feel rich. Perspective determines how we evaluate both ourselves and our circumstances. And if we are humble enough to acknowledge that our point of view might be less than perfect, we can almost always find reasonable and less disturbing judgments of ourselves and whatever happens to us. And once we have identified a more positive alternative perspective, devoting our *selective attention* to it can help us rein in catastrophic thinking and diminish emotional distress.

Humility is required for positive change, including that which results from focused positivity. Before we are likely to search for functional alternative thoughts, we must first acknowledge that our perspective—the collection of assumptions we make about the world—might be improved. This can be a challenging proposition, however, because past events considered in retrospect seem so "predictable" that the illusion is created that we should also be able to predict the future. As a result, we can be unrealistically confident of our views and reluctant to replace them.

It can be comforting to think we know what is coming tomorrow, but none of us really does. As Yankee great Yogi Berra once said, "It's tough to make predictions, especially about the future." Our ideas about the future are filled with illusion—fantasy created by our imagination to accommodate our fears and wishes. As our thoughts about what will happen are largely illusory, it makes sense for us to search for alternatives that inspire hope and constructive action and enhance our peace of mind. Focusing on functional thoughts can help us relax and respond more effectively to the challenges immediately in front of us. In a world where, apart from death and taxes, nothing is guaranteed or certain, *absolute thinking*—the notion that things must be just one particular way—is often counterproductive.

To paraphrase an eminent astrophysicist, scientific investigation has determined that the universe is not only weirder than we might have supposed but weirder than we *can* suppose. Reality is mysterious and confusing and our ability to understand or control it is limited. We are primate cousins of the chimpanzee but much weaker, slower, and less agile. On the other hand, we are the marvels who have conquered Earth and space. Depending on our perspective—how we choose to look at things—we are inadequate apes or paragons of the universe. Given our inherent fallibility and the overwhelming complexity of life, it is surprising that so many of us take for granted the accuracy of our automatic assumptions and are reluctant to consider alternative views.

Some have argued that ignoring disturbing thoughts may represent an unhealthy—and possibly dangerous—denial of reality. Repression— simply blotting out and forgetting upsetting thoughts and feelings—is generally considered an immature and ineffective way of coping with adversity. Without at least occasionally setting aside and ignoring disturbing concerns, however, life would be overwhelming. Deliberately suppressing a counterproductive thought in favor of a more functional idea can be necessary for us to meet everyday obligations and manage personal affairs. Shifting the focus of our attention to thoughts more likely to inspire or reassure often represents our best hope for getting something done, as well as enhancing our peace of mind.

SOMETHING BETTER IS JUST A FEW "STEPS" AWAY

Even those of us who have been treated worst by life retain the capacity to pursue greater knowledge, expand and enrich personal relationships, express ourselves, improve our self-care routines, and engage in activities that can enhance our sense of meaning or purpose. We can respond to feelings of hopelessness and helplessness by living one day at a time, letting go of all that is beyond our control, and shifting the focus of our attention to what we can control. We can take steps to repair ourselves and to create experiences that can compensate us for the pain we endured. We can strive to make life more meaningful and rewarding—and to attain greater peace of mind in the process.

We are never completely helpless because there is always some potentially constructive action we can take. When we feel discouraged or hopeless, we can:

Watch a TV show
Call or visit someone likely to have a positive influence
Read something inspirational or at least distracting
Take a walk
Read or (even better) listen to a meditation induction
Listen (or even better dance) to our preferred music
Write about our experiences or feelings
Peruse a recreation department or community college course catalog
Begin constructing a family tree
Visit an interesting or relaxing place in the community (for example, a museum, park, pier, etc.)
Inquire about volunteer opportunities at a hospital, nursing home, library, or community theater
Review or (even better) add to your *Record of Functional Thought*
Follow a recommended step toward greater peace of mind

PATIENCE

Changes in our habits of behaving and thinking are much more likely to last if they occur gradually. Occasionally we can swiftly make a major life change, such as when we leave an abusive relationship or enter a detox/rehab facility. More often, however, our chances of steering our life in a desired direction depend on persistence in pursuing gradual changes without any dramatic immediate payoff. In other words, our challenge is to persevere at "nudging" our life circumstances toward our goal.

Once we have identified a counterproductive behavior pattern, we can begin taking steps to replace it with a healthier alternative. The keys to success are setting reachable goals, gradually expanding our original goal by achievable increments, tolerating "slip-ups," adjusting our goals in response to setbacks, and persisting. The less complicated the plan, the more likely we are to stick with it long enough to succeed.

Making a daily schedule can help us complete a change plan. The schedule should include our usual daily routines (for example, meals, bedtime, appointments, etc.) as well as other goal activities, such as exercise, creative or self-expressive activities, and opportunities for expending our interpersonal or community involvement.

A GOOD IDEA BADLY APPLIED

Norman Vincent Peale's *The Power of Positive Thinking* is one of the most widely read self-help books of all time. Some of the ideas he expressed, however, are of questionable validity, inconsistent with conventional religious belief, and offensive to many. Although almost certainly popular among his well-to-do Manhattan parishioners, Peale's suggestion that good health and financial wealth indicate who God most favors (known as "prosperity gospel") is particularly disturbing. Also troubling is Peale's advocacy of the "gnostic heresy," the idea that the *intuitions* of those who have been "chosen" reveal "God's will" and, therefore, represent "Truth." These two perversions of Christian teachings have been used to justify disrespect for those of us who have been less fortunate and to create "alternative facts," ideas contradicted by scientific and historical evidence but adhered to nonetheless because they are convenient and self-justifying. Although focusing on thoughts such as these might improve the emotional experience of those of us who have been fortunate, neither is justified nor plays a crucial role in focused positivity's ability to enhance our peace of mind.

Every major religion, from Islam to Judaism to Hinduism to Buddhism to secular humanism, calls for mutual understanding, respect, and compassion. Ideas that separate us from one another are considered counterproductive for humankind in general, whereas those that highlight our commonalities and connections are believed to improve our world. Unfortunately, some of the ideas put forth by Peale have been used divisively.

Even ideas that are generally constructive can be misinterpreted and misused, and any change technique might be perverted to justify corrupt thoughts and bad acts. On a personal level, nevertheless, focusing our attention on positive thoughts creates the best opportunity for us to enhance our success in life and our peace of mind.

COMPASSION

Messages posted by successful people and popular influencers are often designed to motivate (for example, "Step toward success," "Choose good habits," "Just do it!," "Just say no!," etc.). Maxims of this type are rarely helpful, however, because they are based on two false premises:

1. that we would always be successful if only we tried harder, and
2. that we could (and should) know *how*—and have the means—to be more successful.

For many of us, improving our life is a complicated proposition. Simple "pick yourself up by the bootstraps" messages overlook the critical role that luck can play in anyone's outcomes. Many of us have not had sufficient good fortune in our biology, family, community, state, and country to possess the hope, knowledge, and resources that can be required for "success." It is all too easy for those who have turned their good fortune into success to attribute inequity to the inferiority or moral corruption of others, essentially *blaming the victim* instead of advocating for providing the tools and resources that would be likely to foster greater success.

Because we are human, we sometimes cannot help but interpret the outcomes of our actions on the "shame-pride continuum." This view, however, overlooks the major role usually played by factors we had nothing to do with (for example, genetics, early experience, circumstances, the actions of others, etc.). When events and circumstances go our way, *gratitude* is not only a more appropriate response than pride but also one that is more likely to improve our outlook. When things do not go our way, humility can help us recognize the limits of our control, curb our sense of shame, and preserve our sense of dignity.

TAKING GREATER CONTROL

Life is what we make of it—both literally and figuratively. Literally because we can use our voice and our energy to influence others and shape the world to be more as we would like it. Figuratively because even without changing anything in the world around us, we can still find alternative perspectives that make the events and circumstances of our lives more palatable just as they are. A blend of these two approaches, combined with narrowing the focus of our attention to what is possible in the immediate moment, provides us the best opportunity to enhance our peace of mind.

The central message of this book is that we can all profit by learning to

1. recognize and invest our energy in improving those aspects of our lives we can change,
2. become mindful of dysfunctional thoughts that spoil our motivation and mood,
3. respond to dysfunctional thoughts by identifying reasonable alternative ideas more likely to inspire hope and constructive action, and
4. selectively focus our attention on these functional alternatives.

SOME FINAL FUNCTIONAL THOUGHTS

By using my power to shift the focus of my attention, I can improve both my outcomes and my state of mind.

By finding and focusing on thoughts that inspire or reassure, I can enhance my motivation and peace of mind.

By recognizing what I can't control, understanding that I'm only human, and giving myself credit for whatever I've managed to accomplish, I will be able to forgive my "failures" and feel better about myself.

By recognizing thoughts that inhibit me from taking reasonable actions and focusing on functional alternatives, I will be able to speak up for myself more, assume greater control over the direction of my life, feel less helpless, develop greater self-assurance, and enrich the quality of my experience.

By better appreciating the importance of personal relationships and better understanding how I can improve them, I will be able to enhance my feeling of connection to others.

By practicing techniques for calming down, I will be able to improve my health and decision making.

By learning how to create the illusion of willpower and better understanding the factors that control my behavior, I will be able to develop healthier habits.

By improving my personal connections, seeking greater knowledge and understanding, and engaging in self-expressive activities, I can enhance my feelings of belonging and purpose.

I never lose the capacity to alter my perspective, influence my circumstances, and shape my future.

Every new moment can be a "turning point" from which I make my life more purposeful and fulfilling.

Bibliography

Abumrad, Jad. *Radiolab: Investigating a Strange World*. Radio Podcast, WNYC, NPR, 2003–Present.

Adams, Douglas. *A Hitchhiker's Guide to the Galaxy*. New York: Del Rey (a division of Random House), 1979.

Alberti, Robert, and Michael Emmons. *Your Perfect Right: Assertiveness and Equality in Your Life and Relationships*. Tenth edition. Oakland, CA: Impact Publishers, 2017 (first edition published in 1971).

Alcoholics Anonymous. *The Big Book*. Original Edition, 1939.

Asimov, Isaac. *I, Robot*. New York: Random House, 1950.

Atkinson, John, and David McClelland. *The Principles of Learning*. 1953 (out of print textbook).

Beattie, Melodie. *Codependent No More*. Center City, MN: Hazelden, 1986.

Benson, Herbert. *The Relaxation Response*. New York: Morrow and Co., Inc., 1975.

Bryson, Bill. *A Short History of Almost Everything*. New York: Random House, 2003.

Chernow, Ronald. *Alexander Hamilton*. New York: The Penguin Group, 2004.

Christian, David. *Origin Story: A Big History of Everything*. New York: The Hachette Book Group, 2018.

Cover, Robert. *One Hundred Dollar Misunderstanding*. Berkeley, CA: Creative Arts Books, 1962.

Diamond, Jared. *Guns, Germs, and Steel: The Fates of Human Societies.* New York: W. W. Norton and Co., 1997.

Dubner, Stephen J. *Freakonomics: The Hidden Side of Everything.* Radio Podcast, NY, WNJP, NPR, 2010–Present.

Eagleman, David. *Incognito: The Secret Lives of the Brain.* New York: Vintage Books, 2012 (originally published by Canongate Books Ltd., Edinburgh, 2011).

Ellis, Albert, and Ron A. Harper. *A Guide to Rational Living.* New York: Institute for Rational Living, 1961.

Ellison, Ralph. *Invisible Man.* New York: Random House, 1952.

Ferster, C. B., and B. F. Skinner. *Schedules of Reinforcement.* Upper Saddle River, NJ: Prentice Hall, 1957.

Freidman, Sonya. *Men Are Just Desserts.* New York: Warner Books, 1994.

Freud, Sigmund. *The Psychopathology of Everyday Life.* Berlin: Monograph for Psychiatry and Neurology, 1901.

Gawande, Atul. *Being Mortal: Medicine and What Matters in the End.* New York: Metropolitan Books, 2014.

Grant, Adam. *Think Again.* New York: Viking Press, 2021.

Greene, Brian. *The Elegant Universe: Superstrings, Hidden Dimensions, and the Quest for the Ultimate Theory.* New York: Random House, 2003.

Harari, Yuval N. *Sapiens: A Brief History of Humankind.* London: Havril Secker, 2014 (first published in Hebrew in Israel in 2010).

Harris, Thomas A. *I'm Okay, You're Okay.* New York: Harper and Row, 1967.

Hawking, Stephen. *A Brief History of Time.* New York: Bantom Books, 1988.

Heinlen, Robert A. *Stranger in a Strange Land.* New York: G. P. Putnam's Sons, 1961.

Heller, Joseph. *Catch 22.* New York: Simon & Schuster, 1961.

Herbert, Frank. *Dune.* Boston: Chilton Books, 1965.

Hugo, Victor. *Les Misérables.* Belgium: A. Lacroix, Verboeckhoven and Cie, 1862.

Huxley, Aldous. *Brave New World.* London: Chatto and Windus, 1932.

Jacobson, Edmund. *Progressive Relaxation.* Chicago: University of Chicago Monographs in Medicine, 1938.

Kabat-Zinn, Jon. *Full Catastrophe Living: Using the Wisdom of Your Body and Mind to Face Stress, Pain, and Illness.* New York: Bantam Books, 1990.

Kahneman, Daniel. *Thinking Fast and Slow.* New York: Farrar, Straus and Giroux, 2011.

Lange, A. J. *Responsible Assertive Behavior: Cognitive/Behavioral Procedures for Trainers*. Champaign, IL: Research Press, 1978.

LeGuin, Ursula K. *The Lathe of Heaven*. New York: Scribner, 1971.

Levitt, Steven D., and Stephen J. Dubner. *Freakonomics: A Rogue Economist Explores the Hidden Side of Everything*. New York: HarperCollins, 2005.

Louwen, James W. *Lies My Teacher Told Me: Everything Your American History Textbook Got Wrong*. New York: The New Press, 1995.

Malcolm X, as told to Alex Haley. *The Autobiography of Malcolm X*. New York: Ballantine Publishing, 1964.

McGilchrest, Iain. *The Master and His Emissary*. London: Hobbs, 2010.

Miller, Lulu. *Why Fish Don't Exist: A Story of Loss, Love, and the Hidden Order of Life*. New York: Simon & Schuster, 2020.

Morris, Desmond. *The Naked Ape*. New York: Random House, 1967.

Newport, Cal. *Deep Work: Rules for Focused Success in a Distracted World*. New York: Grand Central Publishing, 2016.

Okawa, Ryuho. *The Essence of Buddha*. London: Time Warner Books, 2002.

Orwell, George. *1984*. London: Secker and Warburg, 1949.

Perls, Fritz. *In and Out the Garbage Pail*. Goldsboro, ME: Gestalt Journal Press, 1992.

Pinker, Steven. *Enlightenment Now: The Case for Reason, Science, Humanism, and Progress*. New York: Penguin Books, 2018.

Pohl, Frederik. *Gateway*. New York: St. Martin's Press, 1977.

Pronin, Emily, Daniel Y. Lin, and Lee Ross. "The Blind Spot: Perceptions in Bias in Self Versus Others." *Personality and Social Psychology Bulletin* 28, no. 3 (2002).

Sacks, David. *The Man Who Mistook His Wife for a Hat: And Other Clinical Tales*. New York: Tombstone, 1970.

Sapolsky, Robert M. *Behave: The Biology of Humans at Our Best and Worst*. New York: Penguin Press, 2017.

Steinbeck, John. *The Grapes of Wrath*. New York: Viking Press, 1939.

Thaler, Richard H. *Nudge: Improving Decisions About Health, Wealth, and Happiness*. New York: Penguin Books, 2009.

Vedantam, Shanker. *Hidden Brain: A Conversation About Life's Hidden Patterns*. Radio Podcast, NY, Hidden Brain Media, 2015–Present.

Vonnegut, Kurt. *Slaughterhouse-Five*. New York: Random House, 1969.

Wood, Wendy. *Good Habits, Bad Habits*. New York: Farrar, Straus and Giroux, 2019.

Zinn, Howard. *A People's History of the United States*. New York: HarperCollins, 1980.

Index

About the Author

Dr. John F. Tholen is a retired clinical psychologist who studied at UCLA and the University of Miami before practicing psychology in Southern California for more than forty years. He and his wife, Sandy, a retired attorney and nurse practitioner, now split their time between homes in Long Beach, California, and Austin, Texas, now home to both of their sons and their two grandchildren. Dr. Tholen has published one prior book, *Winning the Disability Challenge*. His primary interests are family, friends, bicycling, kayaking, and duplicate bridge.